HOW TO COPE SUCCESSFULLY WITH

STRESS

ANNA RUSHTON

Wellhouse Publishing Ltd

First published in Great Britain in 2004 by
Wellhouse Publishing Ltd
31 Middle Bourne Lane
Lower Bourne
Farnham, Surrey GU10 3NH

DISCLAIMER

The aim of this book is to provide general information only and
should not be treated as a substitute for the medical advice of
your doctor or any other health care professional. The publisher
and author is not responsible or liable for any diagnosis made by
a reader based on the contents of this book. Always consult your
doctor if you are in any way concerned about your health.

A catalogue record for this book is available from the British Library

ISBN 1 903784 18 2

Printed and bound in Great Britain by
Creative Print & Design Group, Middlesex UB7 0LW

Contents

About the author

Anna Rushton is a well-respected and prolific author, freelance health writer and columnist covering a variety of health-related subjects. Anna is a certified lifestyle coach with a common-sense approach to stress, based in East Sussex she runs workshops and seminars throughout the UK.

Introduction

If you believe you are suffering from stress, then you are certainly not alone. In a survey undertaken in October 2003, 70 per cent of the UK population believed themselves to be suffering from stress – a figure that increases to 88 per cent among 25–34 year-olds; 83 per cent for 35–44 year-olds; and 81 per cent for 45–54 year-olds. Those figures apply to all of us, and with the increased pace and change that we are all experiencing in society it is likely to increase unless we take some action.

Stress at work is also on the increase; the Stress and Health at Work (SHAW) study conducted in 1995 estimated that one in five of the British working population, or approximately five million people, believed their job was extremely or very stressful. Nor is this a new phenomenon, as a 1995 Stress and Health and Work Study indicated that ill health stemming from work-related stress is the second biggest cause of occupational ill health in Great Britain and was costing between £3.7 billion and £3.8 billion every year at 1995/96 prices. If it was like that in 1995, how much more is it costing society today?

Stress is a word that is much used to describe a variety of conditions, and it is likely that all of us will suffer from one or other stress symptoms at some point in our lives. Perhaps some will be affected more frequently or more severely than others, but no one is immune. If at least one in five of the population believe themselves to be, or are diagnosed as being, stressed we can appreciate that this is a problem on a vast scale. Here is a very significant number of people whose lives are being subjected to a range of effects from minor inconvenience to major disruption to health and well-being.

At its root, stress is all about change and how we respond to it. We certainly live in a society whose hallmark is rapid change, and what seemed unthinkable and science fiction fantasies 100 years ago is now an everyday part of our lives. The last century saw the advent of radio, television, computers, automobiles, mobile phones, motorcycles, propeller aeroplanes, jet aircraft, space ships, a moon landing, test-tube babies, two wars which involved the entire Earth in conflict, nuclear power generation and nuclear weapons.

Rapid change means high stress levels and we have not all necessarily moved at the same pace as the technological world around us. In this environment, as we grow older we can no longer be assured of having the 'right answer' to every problem to pass on to our children, as some of them are ideas or situations we have not even encountered before. Life is changing radically within the space of even one generation. The emphasis is on 'youth culture', where flexibility and adaptability to change are vital if one is to 'stay on top'. A continuously changing life can also increase stress in both young people, who feel they can't keep up, and the older generation, who feel they don't have the skills to thrive in today's society where flexibility and adaptability are the most valued characteristics.

Your body will respond automatically to stress and because there are so many causes, both internal and external, one of the most helpful things we can consider is how to manage stress to minimize its effects. If we can't control the stressful events in our lives, what we can try to control is our response to it as it seems very unlikely we can actually eradicate it from our lives altogether.

What is important is finding out just what triggers stress for you and you alone. Missing your usual train home is certainly stressful, but if you meet an old friend at the station and spend the next hour having a coffee and catching up, then the stress level could be greatly reduced. On the other hand, if you have promised to be home in time to go to the cinema with the family, then that hour's delay could be highly stressful. Missing the train is neutral; it is our response to it that either will or will not be stressful. Losing your job is the most stressful thing many of us can imagine, but again for some people it is a new challenge and the start of a whole new way of life.

Not all stress is bad. It can have positive effects in stirring us to action and keeping us motivated and energized. Our bodies are designed by nature to deal with stress: our 'fight or flight' response comes from a very positive desire for self-preservation, and stress in a dangerous situation can be beneficial as it heightens our senses and forces us to full alertness. It is finding the right balance that makes all the difference.

What we are going to be looking at is what stress is in general terms; the physical and mental effects and what stress can lead to if left unchecked. Once we can identify what causes us personally to feel stressed – there are some useful checklists and questionnaires to help you do that – then we can decide whether we want to talk to our doctor, our pharmacist, an alternative therapist or take some self-help measures. Or in fact try a combination of several of these methods, because one of the main attributes of stress is that it definitely responds to a multi-disciplinary approach. So we will examine all the help that is available from self-help measures to medication. The important thing to remember is that stress is common to all of us and that we deal with it most effectively when we know more about what stress is and what our own personal triggers are.

First of all, if you are at all concerned about any aspect of your health, do check with your doctor before embarking on any change in your healthcare regime or following any of the suggestions in this book.

Chapter One

What is Stress?

Stress is a word that is used frequently, but what exactly is it? Simply put, anything that makes you anxious, frustrated, unhappy, angry or tense can make you stressed and if you don't handle that stress well then your health can be affected. Stress affects virtually all of us, and as well as the emotional and psychological disruption it causes, stress-related medical problems are becoming increasingly common. Today, we all need to learn how to cope with stress.

Almost anything can make us feel stressed, but essentially there are six key triggers that are common for most people:

1   separation and loss, such as losing our job, getting divorced or the death of someone close;

2   being stuck or frustrated in a situation we feel powerless to change, such as being passed over for promotion or stuck in traffic when we are late for an appointment;

3   a major new life event which puts us in an unknown situation, such as moving house, going to a new school or job;

4   the unpredictability of situations, such as company mergers, taking exams, or any situation where change is inevitable but we cannot be sure of the outcome;

5   tensions that arise from the demands of conflicting situations, such as working full time and running a home, looking after a sick or elderly family member while running your own business or holding down a full-time job;

6   emotional conflict from doing something that you either don't like or feel uncomfortable with, such as working in a job you hate, being the odd one out in your social circle if behaviour over things like drugs or alcohol don't match your own standards.

There are of course ways of establishing how stressed you are, and we will look at that more deeply in Chapter Four.

Fight or Flight

Our body's response to stress is automatic, and pre-determined. You don't have to think about how to react because your body has already gone into full danger and alert mode. If you have been jostled or bumped in the street or a queue then, automatically, your body goes into 'fight or flight' mode, which we can identify as stress. In response to the perceived threat your blood pressure rises, your pulse quickens and you breathe more rapidly. In fact all your senses go on to full alert and stay that way until the pressure is released. If you are being threatened by a mugger, then the stress is necessary to help you cope and your body stays on alert. If you recognize the other person as a friend or see that they didn't mean to jostle you, then your body returns to normal and no harm is done and all your physical responses gradually return to normal.

It is not an isolated incident that usually causes us problems, but if our body is continually being stressed, and there is no proper recovery time between episodes, then that can lead to problems. People who are faced with this can then end up feeling exhausted because frequent production of the hormone cortisol will depress the immune system, and a healthy immune system is vital for overall well-being. We will find out more about the chemical processes in our body in response to stress in the next chapter, but first let's concentrate on what stress means to each individual.

External and Internal Stressors

Stress occurs when you are worried about major life changes like redundancy, unemployment or retirement, or concerned that you can't pay your bills, or anxious about your own health or that of a close family member or friend. If it is something that makes you worry, then it is stressful, but this definition relies just on your response to external events. Your body sees things rather differently because physically stress means change and anything that causes a change in your life causes stress.

Do you recognize any of these situations as being potentially stressful?

- Promotion at work
- Your car has a flat battery
- A birthday party that lasts till 3.00 a.m.
- Your pet is ill and needs an operation
- The delivery of some new furniture
- Friends or family coming to stay
- An outbreak of spots or an allergic reaction.

This list may seem a little odd to you. Why would going to a party, getting a promotion or having new furniture be stressful? Generally we think that it is only these situations that cause us worry and anxiety that are going to be stressful, but even good situations can stress us. Take the promotion for instance. Yes, it is great to be acknowledged and rewarded, but you may also have to work longer hours which could put a strain on your family relationships or you may have some secret concerns about how well you may cope. Even that party can be stressful if you stay up way beyond your usual bedtime and eat and drink more than usual, because physically your body is stressed by having to cope with the change in circumstances. Plus, if you are wondering if you are alert enough to drive, or anxious about whether you will get up in time for work, then that too can be stressful. As you can see, it doesn't matter if it the change is 'good' or 'bad' because in either case it provokes a response in us. For example, buying your ideal home is a wonderful thing, but moving is one of the most stressful events we can undertake. We face these kinds of dualities every day, often without being consciously aware of how much stress we are putting ourselves under.

Stress or Excitement?

We are all affected differently by the events in our lives, and what is stressful to one might be exciting to another. For instance, planning a big wedding or making a speech may be exhilarating and pleasurable to one person and highly worrying and fearsome to another. So it is not necessarily the events themselves that cause us the greatest stress, but how we react to them. In fact, certain levels of stress are essential to motivate us and are also a key element in our survival. We do need to be alert to the dangers around us, and without the stimulus of stress we do not always perform at our best or to our greatest potential.

Stress is many different kinds of things: an emotional response to happy and sad events, physical reaction to danger, and mental stress from feeling overburdened and unable to cope. Many people have huge amounts of stress in their daily lives without really being aware of it. It is only when the stress continues over a period of time that the results become obvious and have to be dealt with.

Stress is a response to change, but it doesn't need to be real and actual change to provoke a stressful reaction. Anyone who has lain awake at night worrying about what might happen or could possibly occur will know just how stressful that 'imagined change' can be. Imagined changes are just as stressful as real ones, and there are several types of stress that we can identify.

Emotional Stress

When our relationships are going smoothly, at home and at work, then we are in a fairly stress-free zone. However, if we are subject daily to tensions, arguments, disagreements and conflicts that we don't feel either in charge of or comfortable with, then that is extremely stressful. If you are a naturally shy person and your job requires you to be in front of the public all the time, or you are on the receiving end of pressure and verbal aggression from customers, then it is hard to imagine anything more stressful. Ask any parent about the ongoing arguments with their children about boundaries, tidiness and a hundred other things and ask if that is stressful? Some parents will take it in their stride as a normal part of family life, especially if it is the kind of family life that they are used to from their own childhood, but others can be distressed and upset by the rows and fights if their early family environment was very different.

Have you ever apologized for someone else's behaviour or tried to take responsibility for their actions or non-actions? If your partner doesn't like parties and refuses to go or stands sulkily in a corner all night you may well try to compensate for their behaviour by working harder at being extra social to make up for them, and if that isn't natural to you, it will be stressful. If your colleague at work hasn't done their share of the work and you don't want to look inefficient in front of the boss, you may take responsibility for their actions so as to present a better picture of your work skills. You will probably also be resentful and angry, both stressful emotions. Taking responsibility for someone else is a major stressor because ultimately you don't have control over someone else's life and can't predict the outcome. The emotional toll can be heavy in trying either to apologize for their behaviour or to compensate for what you see as their inadequacies or failures to carry out the things they have agreed to.

The Physical Load
In our society we set a great store by hard work and success is often measured in how long you have been in the office or how much work you take home in the evenings or at weekends. We are working longer and longer hours and the demands on our time are greater than ever before. New technology, such as the rapid rise in emails and our constant availability on mobile phones, has increased the workload hugely for many people. All this extra work is depriving your body of balance; it needs time to rest and recover in order to carry out the essential internal maintenance and repair work that is needed to keep you functioning healthily. Working long hours reduces the time you have available to do that. This means you are constantly in deficit to your body because you are draining out more energy than you are replacing. Sooner or later that catches up with you and manifests itself as stress as your body tries to keep you healthy, but without the back up and support it needs from you.

Your Daily Environment
Even a simple thing like a change in temperature can cause your body stress that it has to react to. This is because change of any kind, however minor, can be stressful. Even the pleasure of going on holiday (which carries its own stresses for many people) to a very hot, or cold, climate forces your body to adapt and draw on huge reserves to cope with this difference. Everyday traffic fumes and toxins in the environment cause your body to work harder to filter them out and again can be stressful. If you work in a very warm centrally-heated office, then travel home on an unheated

train or bus, again your body is forced to respond to the change and that puts it under stress.

Cigarettes and Smoking
Smoking is certainly bad for your health, and one of the reasons lies in the fact that tobacco is in itself a powerful toxin. The combination of chemicals released when a cigarette is lit destroys the cells that clean your trachea, bronchi and lungs. The carbon monoxide from cigarette smoking causes chronic carbon monoxide poisoning and long-term cigarette smoking causes damage to the arteries in your body, causing insufficient blood supply to the brain, heart and vital organs. All this puts a huge stress on your body as it tries to combat the damage.

Allergic Stress
Allergic reactions are a natural part of your body's defence mechanism as it tries to protect you from a foreign substance. If your body is presented with something which it considers to be toxic, then it will do its very best to get rid of it by either attacking it or neutralizing its effect. Ever wondered why you get a runny nose in summer? If pollen gets into your nose, your body will throw up an immediate defence to expel it through sneezing or a runny nose. If you have tried a new shampoo or soap and your skin gets dry and itchy, that is the allergic defence your body puts up to get the substance outside the body and onto the skin as it tries to stop you using it again. If you have eaten a food you are allergic to, then you may come out in a rash. So you can see that an allergic reaction requires the body to change its normal mode of operation and go into rescue or emergency session. This requires a lot of energy and is stressful.

There are, as you can see, many ways of defining stress and many reasons why ourbody responds with a stressful reaction. What we need to find out is exactly what stress means for us personally, so that we can begin to tackle it.

ChapterTwo

The Chemical Connection

We have looked at how our 'fight or flight' mechanism automatically comes into play when we are faced with danger. This response triggers a whole range of bodily changes in order to provide us with the means to either run away or stand and fight our corner. This reflex is governed by our autonomic nervous system and is something we have no control over. This is the involuntary system that keeps our heart beating and our lungs working all the time, awake or asleep. We don't have to think about breathing – it is automatic. There are two parts to the autonomic nervous system, the sympathetic and the parasympathetic nerves, and they have totally different and opposite actions. When we are alarmed our heart rate speeds up and that is the sympathetic nerves in action, and when you are calming down it is the parasympathetic nerves which slow the heart rate to its normal level. The level of our response to danger is governed by these two nerves and it is the balance between them which will determine how actively you deal with any stressful situation.

The Body's Response

When you face danger the sympathetic nervous system goes immediately into action and stimulates your adrenal glands to secrete more of the hormones adrenaline and cortisol. This activity diverts all your other bodily activity away from everyday functions like digestion and directs all its efforts into your muscles so you are ready to run or stand and fight. You will need more energy, so greater amounts of fat and glucose are circulated in the blood and your breathing pattern is likely to become faster and deeper so that you can draw in more oxygen. Your face may look pale because blood is drawn away from non-essential areas like the skin, and your heart rate and blood pressure will rise rapidly.

This rapid increase in hormonal and nervous system activity can also cause diarrhoea or nausea and the mouth to become dry as the saliva glands reduce their non-essential output. Changes also occur in the sweat glands as they increase production, so you may experience a 'cold sweat' on your skin. When in danger the senses we need are sharpened, so our hearing becomes more acute and our pupils expand to take in as much light as possible so that we can see the situation more clearly.

When in a dangerous situation there is always the possibility of injury, so the body prepares itself for the worst by releasing endorphins from the adrenal and pituitary glands as well as the brain to help us deal with any potential pain. Endorphins act like strong painkillers to reduce feeling in the injured area, and also help the blood clot faster to speed up the healing process.

All these are excellent defence mechanisms when faced with a serious threat, but unfortunately they arise just the same whether your life is under attack or someone has trodden on your foot in a lift. There is no regulator, and as we rarely encounter life-threatening attacks, if we are frequently responding on this level then our body literally becomes exhausted. Plus our hormonal balance is upset by having to throw in all its reserves all of the time. When we are stressed this is what we are doing and the reason why those under constant stress feel so tired and drained.

The Brain's Response

If we have been suffering the effects of stress over a continuous period, then there are risks of physical damage to the gastrointestinal tract, glandular system, skin or cardiovascular system as the body tries to cope with the incessant demands made on it. But it is not just in our body that stress manifests itself; prolonged stress also causes physical changes in the brain. Some of the more common symptoms of stress such as depression, anxiety, sleep disturbance, fatigue and outbursts of crying for no reason are caused by a chemical malfunction in the brain. We will look more closely at the symptoms of stress in the next chapter, but let's first look at the way our brain chemicals function and are affected by stress.

Chemical Messengers

Since 1977 scientists have been able to find out about the inner workings of the brain through being able to penetrate into the very interior of single nerve cells. This work revealed that vital chemicals carry messages between brain cells which allow them to communicate with each other. Every day billions of such messages are being sent back and forth between the cells in the brain. There are two different kinds of messengers and the messages they carry are the complete opposite to each other. Their function is either to encourage or inhibit our feelings and behaviour; they are 'positive' messengers and 'negative' messengers. The positive ones send happy, uplifting and joyful messages and the negative messengers carry the less positive, less stimulating and sadder messages. The majority of our nerve centres receive input from both types of messengers and as long as this input is balanced between the two, then everything runs along on an even keel.

There are three positive messengers in the brain: serotonin, noradrenaline and dopamine. It is these brain chemicals that begin to malfunction when stress levels become more than we can handle comfortably. They each have quite different functions, as detailed below.

Seratonin

Serotonin is essential for ensuring that you get a good night's sleep and when we are stressed this is often the first change we notice. If serotonin is out of balance then restful sleep will elude you because it is responsible for the regulation of our internal body clock that makes sure the body is ready and receptive for sleep. The body clock lives at the very centre of the brain in the pineal gland and it is in there that serotonin is stored ready for use by the body. It is actually converted by the body into melatonin every day and then converted back again to serotonin over a 24-hour period, and that is what decides your body clock. This daily cycle is how your body chemistry is adjusted to a sleep and wake pattern so that when it is working optimally, the serotonin will make sure that each night you are drowsy and ready to sleep and maintains the sleep cycle throughout the night so that your sleep is deep and restful. It is the switch to melatonin each morning that means you wake up rested and refreshed.

As well as regulating our sleep patterns, our body clock is also responsible for co-ordinating body temperature. Every 24 hours your body temperature cycles from high to low, varying by as much as one degree. When it is time to wake up and be active, your body temperature rises slightly, and when it is time to fall asleep it drops a little and again it is your body clock that regulates that temperature difference. Another vital element in sleep regulation is the hormone cortisol, which is the body's chief stress-fighting hormone. We have very high cortisol levels when we are in 'fight or flight' mode, but they normally drop dramatically at night as we relax and prepare for sleep. As with body temperature, the natural rise and fall of cortisol in the body must continue on its usual course throughout every 24 hours. However, if you are constantly stressed then this cycle is disrupted and it becomes very difficult to get a proper restful night's sleep.

Noradrenaline

Noradrenaline is responsible for setting the energy levels in the body, and is related to adrenaline. It is one of the positive messengers and is vital to a healthy nervous system. If levels of noradrenaline drop, we don't have enough energy and feel tired and exhausted, with no enthusiasm to do anything. If you feel constantly exhausted and lethargic when stressed, it may be that your level of noradrenaline is out of balance.

Dopamine

Dopamine is the third positive brain messenger and is responsible for both our pleasurable and painful feelings. We produce natural morphine-like molecules in our brains that are known as endorphins, and they regulate our awareness of both pain and pleasure. Dopamine is found in the area of the brain next to where endorphins are released, so if our dopamine messengers fail then our production of endorphins is also threatened. It is stress that causes dopamine failure and if you notice that you are more sensitive to pain than usual that could be a signal that your dopamine messengers are not functioning fully. Dopamine is also responsible for the area of your brain that allows you to enjoy life. When stress interferes with dopamine function the pleasurable messages are no longer being transmitted and things that you normally find enjoyable become dull and uninteresting.

So we can see that when life is running according to plan the positive messages are able to keep up with our needs, but when we are under stress it appears that too many demands are placed on the positive messengers and their ability to keep up with the flow of messages to other cells seems to slow down. If the stress continues, then the positive messages begin to fail. If this happens, then the important nerve centres receive more negative than positive messages and a state of brain chemical imbalance is present. This shift over to more negative than positive brain messengers being sent can result in a sense of being overwhelmed by life, anxious and unable to cope. A common complaint in this situation is a lack of energy and enjoyment of life and often great problems in sleeping.

The Genetic Factor

As we mentioned in the Introduction, everyone's response to stress is different and one of the factors that can affect how you deal with stress may well be genetic. Every one of us inherits the ability to make and use positive messengers, but some people are born with a lower stress tolerance than others. The amount of positive messengers you produce has an effect on how you deal with stress. The more positive messengers you have then the more likely you are to find stress stimulating and challenging and might even feel bored without it. As we have seen, once stress mounts up the number of positive messengers declines and the amount of stress that you can tolerate before your positive messengers malfunction shows your stress tolerance level. This is determined by your genetic inheritance from your parents, and the majority of us inherit a high enough level to enable us to cope with the stress and strain of daily life. Even if you have an average or a high predisposition to tolerate stress, you will probably still experience some of the symptoms of the brain chemical imbalance at key stress points in your life. For the average person this may only come as a response to difficult situations, such as the sleepless nights before an important interview or exam, or facing the extreme pressure of the terminal illness and death of someone close to you. You may not be someone who 'normally' cries but find yourself weeping without reason and this is a sign that the brain chemical balance is not functioning at its normal rate. However, there are estimated to be at least 1 in 10 of the population who have inherited a low stress tolerance and whose positive messengers fail much earlier than the average. Situations which many people would consider marginally stressful, or very low on the stress scale, will have a greater impact on them and can mean they are over stressed and overwhelmed much of the time. Ten per cent of a population is a considerable number of people who are not able to cope with the stress of daily life.

Adjusting Your Brain Chemistry

If we are feeling out of balance our natural instinct is to try to do something to make it better. This usually involves us trying either to stimulate or to sedate our senses with things like coffee, alcohol, sugar, tobacco and drugs. Many of these solutions will work in the short term, but if your system is over stressed they are not the answer for long-term stress-free living. We will look at some of the many self-help and medical remedies available for stress in later chapters, but here is a brief overview on the most commonly used substances that will temporarily increase positive brain messengers. The first one is produced naturally in our bodies; the others are external stimulants.

Adrenaline
Adrenaline is released from the adrenal glands and is our own natural stimulant. If you have ever fallen asleep at the wheel and then jerked awake, you will remember the rush of adrenaline that floods your system and ensures all your senses are on alert. Adrenaline is highly stimulating and addictive for many people; workaholics for instance or those who engage in dangerous sports thrive on the stress and the 'rush' they get from this natural pick-me-up. Adrenaline certainly increases the positive messengers in a dramatic way, but again there is usually a steep crash afterwards

which ultimately stresses the body even further.

Sugar
Sugar is rapidly absorbed into the body and you get a sudden rise in blood sugar levels which gives an immediate boost to the positive messengers. That is why we reach for a sugary snack, chocolate bar or biscuit when we are feeling low. However, it is only a temporary fix because it is always followed by a corresponding fall in the sugar levels. This sets off a vicious cycle, where you keep putting in more sugar to avoid the crash feeling. It is not a tactic that helps your body balance out stress and is only a very short-term fix.

Caffeine
Caffeine is a highly popular pick-me-up and is used to raise energy levels or to stay awake longer than our body wants to. It boosts the positive messengers and whether taken as coffee, cola or chocolate again gives only a short-term boost, followed by the same type of crash we get from sugar.

Alcohol
Drinking alcohol helps the body clock function, which in turn can help people with poor sleep patterns get a few hours' rest, but not the deep natural sleep that we need. Its effects on behaviour can range from initial energy and euphoria to aggression and maudlin sentimentality. It can give a false sense of confidence and certainly increases the body's ability to tolerate pain. Again, it is a short-term fix with potentially disastrous long-term consequences for health if taken in excess.

Tobacco
Smoking cigarettes produces a complex chemical compound, one function of which is to increase positive brain messengers and produce a relaxed state in the body. Many stressed individuals find that cigarettes 'calms their nerves', but again there are serious long-term health consequences associated with tobacco.

One thing that is noticeable about using external stimulants to change our brain chemistry is that they are rarely used in isolation.

21

Smoking, drinking, taking sugar or caffeine may all occur regularly throughout the day to try to artificially boost the number of positive messengers getting through to our brain. However, you cannot accurately rebalance your brain messengers in this way. Your body needs to make this delicate chemical adjustment itself, and we will look at some of the ways you can help it to do that in the self-help chapters.

ChapterThree

Identifying the Signs of Stress

As we have already seen, stress means different things to different people. However, there are some symptoms and conditions that are common to those under stress. For instance, there usually tends to be one or more symptoms or series of symptoms that keep regularly occurring as our personal body response when we are stressed.

The first thing that happens is that our immune system is compromised and we become more prone to infections and illnesses. Our symptoms may be physical, mental or emotional or a mixture of all three. Some of the most common responses to stress are headaches, digestive upsets and a noticeable change in our moods and emotional balance. Feelings of not being able to cope, of being under too much pressure are very common and can result in our becoming weepy, irritable and more moody and short-tempered than is usual for us.

What is very noticeable when we are stressed is that it is difficult to keep things in proportion because they seem so much bigger, or more serious or less bearable than usual. Minor incidents and upsets assume an importance and significance that they would not normally have for us. For instance, your children may not want to get out of bed on a Saturday morning, or your colleague may have got in late again leaving you to deal with the work. Instead of taking it in your stride you may lose your temper or even feel tearful and overwhelmed.

In other words you need to notice where your normal patterns of behaviour are changing. If there are major changes to your eating or sleeping patterns or if you start getting a bit obsessive about things such as whether you have locked the door, then that is an indicator that your stress levels may be high. In the next chapter we look at how you rank in the stress ratings, but first let us look at what effects stress will have in your everyday life and see where you might identify with some of them.

Physical and Emotional Symptoms of Stress

Stress can lead to high blood pressure, migraines, hair loss, mouth ulcers, asthma, panic attacks and digestive problems like ulcers, indigestion and irritable bowel syndrome. If you think back to how our body responds to a stressful situation, by pumping in extra adrenaline and diverting non-essential functions such as digestion, you can easily see where the problems might arise. These are some physical reactions we can get when under stress:

- rapid or shallow breathing
- nausea
- sweating and/or feeling a 'cold' sweat
- blushing or going white in the face
- tension in the muscles, especially the neck and shoulder
- increased frequency of urination or diarrhoea
- numbness or tingling in the hands or feet
- headaches and migraines
- edgy, nervy feeling in the body
- aching limbs or backache
- trembling or shaking
- sleep problems
- skin dryness or rashes
- dry mouth.

Alongside our physical symptoms are the deeper ones that come from emotional and mental stress. Some of the most common are:

- anxiety
- depression
- moodiness
- disturbed sleeping patterns
- uncharacteristic aggressive behaviour
- withdrawal from seeing people and socializing
- change in eating or drinking habits
- inability to concentrate or focus clearly
- indecisive and unable to make decisions
- negative or highly self-critical
- apathetic to people and events
- in need of reassurance.

No symptom in isolation is a symptom of stress; it is when they occur with unusual frequency or on a regular basis that you may want to discuss it with your doctor. In Chapter Four there is more information on how to check on your stress level and some questionnaires that will help you identify this more easily.

Where is the Weak Link?

Prolonged stress undoubtedly will strain your body and result in some form of illness as the body tries to cope. If you have too much stress in your life it is sensible to address it as early as you can, and one way to do that is to identify in what area you personally are most likely to feel the stress. Not only can you inherit a low stress tolerance, but the area of your body where you are going be hit hardest by stress may also be genetically inherited.

As we have seen, everyone has a different response to stress, but there are some effects that are common to most of us. We know that stress makes allergic conditions worse and for asthmatics can even trigger an attack. If you are shaking uncontrollably or breathing so rapidly that you are hyperventilating and starting to feel dizzy or faint, then these are some of the signs of stress. When our immune system is compromised, as it is when we are stressed, then we are also much more susceptible to conditions and symptoms like these:

- outbursts of irritability or anger
- apathy or depression
- constant worrying and anxiety
- unusual or irrational behaviour
- loss of appetite
- comfort eating
- lack of concentration
- loss of sex-drive
- increased use of stimulants to change the mood
- smoking or drinking more than usual.
- You may also notice some of the most common physical changes:
- excessive tiredness
- skin problems
- new aches and pains resulting from tense muscles
- neck or backache
- tension headaches

- increased pain from arthritis and other conditions
- heart palpitations
- changes in the menstrual cycle, particularly missed periods.

All of these events cause us stress and, to help you identify where your 'weak link' may be, below is a brief checklist of common symptoms. It is also worth noting that research has suggested that men and women respond differently to stress. Women have a tendency to become more withdrawn and depressed, whereas men are more likely to become more irritable and aggressive and can turn to addictive behaviours to blot out the stress.

- *Mental stress*: fatigue, aches and pains, crying spells, depression, anxiety attacks, sleep disturbance.
- *Gastrointestinal tract*: ulcer, cramps and diarrhoea, colitis, irritable bowel.
- *Glandular system*: thyroid gland malfunction.
- *Cardiovascular*: high blood pressure, heart attack, abnormal heart beat, stroke.
- *Skin*: itchy skin rashes, allergic reactions.
- *Immune system*: increased vulnerability to infections.

Post-traumatic Stress

It is not an everyday occurrence, but it is worth mentioning the effects of post-traumatic stress. This can occur after a painful, disturbing or violent experience, such as being involved in a disaster like a train, plane or car crash. It may also be caused by witnessing a death or going through an extremely difficult or traumatic experience, such as witnessing a violent death or disaster, being involved in a serious car crash or surviving a fire.

People suffering from post-traumatic stress may experience any of the symptoms listed previously and they may also feel a mixture of emotions such as fear, shame, depression, guilt or anger because they have survived and others perhaps did not. There may be recurrent memories or images that occupy the waking thoughts, and can lead to nightmares. These feelings can last for weeks, months or even years after the traumatic event that triggered them.

Anxious or Depressed?

Stress affects us all differently and you may be someone whose personality makes you more likely to be worried and anxious when life is stressful, or perhaps feel overwhelmed and have a tendency to depression. The following questions are intended to help give you some insight into what your personal tendency is, but it is not a medical diagnosis, just a guideline which you can use to start looking at your stress behaviour response. Tick as many boxes as feel relevant to you right now:

ANXIETY

I feel tense or wound up:

Most of the time ☐
A lot of the time ☐
Occasionally ☐
Not at all ☐

I feel anxious as if something dreadful is going to happen:

Yes, very strongly ☐
Yes, but it's not too bad ☐
A little, but I am not worried about it ☐
Not at all ☐

Worry thoughts occupy my mind:

Most of the time ☐
A lot of the time ☐
Sometimes, but not too often ☐
Occasionally ☐

I feel comfortable and relaxed:

Most of the time ☐
A lot of the time ☐
Occasionally ☐
Not at all ☐

I get butterflies in my stomach:

Most of the time ☐
A lot of the time ☐
Occasionally ☐
Not at all ☐

I get sudden feelings of panic:

Very often ☐
Quite often ☐
Occasionally ☐
Not at all ☐

I feel restless, as if I want to be on the move:

Very much ☐
Quite a lot ☐
Not very often ☐
Not at all ☐

DEPRESSION

I still enjoy life as much as I used to:

Definitely as much ☐
Not quite as much ☐
Only a little ☐
Hardly at all ☐

I laugh and enjoy the funny side of life:

As much as I always have ☐
Not quite as much as before ☐
Definitely less ☐
Not at all ☐

I feel cheerful:

Most of the time   ☐
Sometimes   ☐
Not often   ☐
Not at all   ☐

I feel as if I have slowed right down:

Nearly all the time   ☐
Very often   ☐
Sometimes   ☐
Not at all   ☐

I have lost interest in how I look:

Definitely   ☐
I don't take as much care as before   ☐
I pay a lot less attention than I used to   ☐
I haven't changed   ☐
Not at all   ☐

I get enjoyment from reading, watching television or listening to the radio:

Often   ☐
Sometimes   ☐
Not very often   ☐
Rarely   ☐

Your answers will indicate whether you tend to be more on the anxiety or depressed side of stress. They are not a diagnosis, nor meant to be taken as such, but are simply intended to show you if your response to the stress in your life right now shows up more as anxiety or depression. You may find that you have a mixture of both anxious and depressed answers; that is not unusual because you are unique, and so is your response to stress.

    If you are clearly more anxious than depressed then that is the area to tackle first by looking at your triggers and finding ways to lower your anxiety levels through some of the methods suggested in this book. If you are more depressed, then it would be a good idea to talk with your doctor about possibly taking a short course of antidepressants to help you tackle your condition more effectively. It is certainly more difficult to motivate yourself to take positive action when you are depressed and this can indeed become a source of stress in itself. Your doctor may suggest medication or counselling, and these taken in conjunction with the suggestions here will help you tackle the problem much more effectively.

Chapter Four

Assessing Your Stress Risk

In the last chapter we examined the symptoms that can arise from being stressed, and now it is time to have a look at some of the major stressful life events that we may encounter. Some events of course are common throughout our lives and are easily recognized as being potential sources of stress: pressure of examinations, work, family and personal relationships, illness, moving house, death, separation and divorce.

So, evidently all of us are at risk of being stressed, but it can depend on how many of these events come upon us, and in what sort of timescale. We have seen that we all have very different responses to a stressful situation; it can be stimulating and motivating for some, and overwhelming and de-motivating for others. Our response to the stressful situations in our life is critical in determining how that stress affects our health. Some people are more resilient and better at dealing with stress than others, and there are some simple questions which can help you identify just how vulnerable you are to stress.

Stress Vulnerability Assessment

This is a simple questionnaire that is just designed to help you identify how vulnerable you are to certain types of stress, and to see if you are someone who is affected perhaps more than the average. Each question requires a simple yes or no, and there are no wrong or right answers. It just is a way of trying to identify how robust, or vulnerable, you may be to the effects of stress. Armed with that knowledge it is easier to see what areas you most need to change, modify or get help with. Answer the questions to reflect how you are feeling right now, rather than how you may have felt in the past or what is your usual pattern of behaviour.

When you are upset or annoyed do you find it difficult to hide your feelings from others? Yes/No

Do you feel very strongly about other people's situation or emotions? Yes/No

If you get bad news do you feel as if you have been punched in the stomach? Yes/No

Are you slow to take action when something is stressful for you? Yes/No

Do you spend time worrying about what other people think of you? Yes/No

If someone else is speaking do you often interrupt them? Yes/No

Are you in the habit of finishing other people's sentences? Yes/No

Are you irritated by indecisiveness in others? Yes/No

Are you a demanding sort of person with high standards? Yes/No

Can you 'switch off' at the end of a busy day? Yes/No

Would you say you were an argumentative sort of person? Yes/No

Does 'anything for a quiet life' describe you? Yes/No

Do interruptions to your normal routine upset you? Yes/No

If someone disagrees with you does it make you anxious? Yes/No

Would you describe yourself as indecisive? Yes/No

Do you feel as if you are a failure? Yes/No

Do other people's opinions really matter to you? Yes/No

Do you make your own needs a priority? Yes/No

Are you happy to let others take the decisions? Yes/No

Do you get easily frightened or confused? Yes/No

Do you worry that something terrible is going to happen to you? Yes/No

Is it hard for you to say no to others? Yes/No

When you do say no are you usually ignored? Yes/No

Do you feel you are not fully appreciated by others? Yes/No

Are you feeling overwhelmed by what you have to do? Yes/No

Have you lost your usual sense of humour? Yes/No

Are you comfortable around new people or situations? Yes/No

Are you a perfectionist? Yes/No

When you start something do you often not finish it? Yes/No

When doing simple everyday tasks do you feel exhausted? Yes/No

Are you having problems with concentration? Yes/No

Do you bite your nails? Yes/No

Are you regularly getting a good night's sleep? Yes/No

Has your interest in sex and intimacy declined?	Yes/No
Do you ever feel as if your heart is racing, and you don't have a heart condition?	Yes/No
Are you physically restless, fidgety or drum your fingers?	Yes/No
Do you get frequent headaches or neck pains?	Yes/No
Are you ever breathless or dizzy when you haven't exerted yourself?	Yes/No
Are your symptoms of stress usually physical, for example, headaches?	Yes/No
Do you put work before relationships?	Yes/No

Now total up the number of times you ticked yes and check your score.

Over 20
This means you are well into the danger zone for stress and need to take immediate action. Look at the answers you ticked yes to and see if they fall into a pattern; are they around self-esteem and confidence, are they predominantly physical signs or emotional responses? Once you know, you can start to think about where you could begin to make changes. The suggestions in Chapter 11 on relaxation will be beneficial and lifestyle changes are probably a must. With a high stress level, it is also sensible to talk to your doctor about having a thorough check-up.

Between 20 and 11
This is a wake-up call for you to look at your overall life, and the nearer you are to the higher end of the scale then the more you will be showing stress on all levels. Start the self-help measures outlined in Chapter 6 and take some action to start bringing control back into your life by addressing the everyday stressors you are prone to.

Between 10 and 4
You are more resilient to stress the lower your score, but keep an eye on where your stress triggers are and look at making yourself less vulnerable. If you know that confrontation or emotional pressure is a problem for you, then look at improving your assertiveness skills and self-confidence.

Between 3 and 0
This is the score of someone who handles stress very well and is resilient in the face of change and challenge. If you want to improve even further, check which questions 'pressed your stress buttons' so that you can address this last bit of imperfection!

External Factors

Once you have a clearer idea of what it is that makes you stressful and what your potential vulnerability to stress is, it is helpful to go a bit deeper. It would be helpful to see if there are also other causes for the stress that you have perhaps not considered because they have happened a while ago, or having been going on for so long that you have almost accepted them as a regular part of your life.

What we are looking for here is to be able to identify whether the stress we are under is temporary or long-term. Short-term stress is something we can usually cope with because we know that once the stressful situation is resolved then we will return to normal, and simple self-help measures like chatting to a friend or taking a break will help relieve the situation for us. It is long-term and continuous stress that is harder to deal with and is potentially much more damaging, both emotionally and psychologically, both for us and for our family and friends.

One of the difficulties with long-term stress is that we start to take it for granted and we often simply don't realize the enormous pressure we are under and the strain that our body and emotions are going through. Our feelings of tiredness, irritability or other symptoms are taken after a time as being our normal behaviour. So it is very helpful to be able to take a dispassionate look at your life right now and see how many major external stressors you are under.

Your External Stress Profile

Having looked at the way in which you perhaps handle stress or react to it, it is also valuable to take a look at overall life events that could also have had an impact and have led to the stress you are suffering now. It's not just about what has happened this week, or in the last month, but over the last year. Our response to stressful events can build up, especially if we don't deal with them as they immediately arise. It is like dropping a stone into a pond, when, after the initial splash, the ripples continue outwards for some time across the water. It is exactly like this with a stressful situation: the immediate response is the splash of reaction and response, but the secondary ripples as your body adjusts to cope with it can continue for at least a year afterwards.

The following table assigns values to each event and at the end you can add up your score to give you an idea of where you are on the stress scale.

STRESS SCORE

1	Death of spouse or partner	100
2	Divorce	60
3	Menopause	60
4	Separation from spouse or partner	60
5	Imprisonment or public disgrace	60
6	Death of close family member	60
7	Serious personal injury or illness	45
8	Marriage or establishing new partnership	45
9	Loss of job	45
10	Marital or relationship reconciliation	40
11	Retirement	40
12	Change in health of immediate family member	40
13	Working for more than 40 hours per week	35
14	Pregnancy or responsibility for a pregnancy	35
15	Sexual difficulties	35
16	Gain of a new family member	35
17	Business or work role change	35
18	Change in financial statu	35
19	Death of a close friend	30
20	Increase in marital or partnership arguments	30
21	Mortgage or loan for a major purpose	25
22	Foreclosure on a mortgage or loan	25
23	Sleeping less than eight hours a night	25
24	Change in responsibilities at work	25
25	Trouble with in-laws or children	25

26	Outstanding personal achievement	25
27	Spouse or partner stops or starts work	20
28	Start or end of school life	20
29	Change in living conditions (visitors in the home, change in roommates, renovating or redecorating house)	20
30	Change in personal habits (diet, exercise, smoking and so on)	20
31	Chronic allergies	20
32	Trouble with boss or colleagues	20
33	Change in work hours or conditions	15
34	Moving to new home	15
35	Premenstrual tension	15
36	Change of school	15
37	Change in religious activity	15
38	Change in social activity (more or less than before)	15
39	Minor financial loan	10
40	Change in frequency of family get-togethers	10
41	Holiday	10
42	Major family celebration (for example, Christmas, wedding)	10
43	Minor violation of the law (for example, parking ticket)	5

TOTAL SCORE: ___

If you have had a year of major upheaval involving perhaps death, divorce or change of home, then that has a serious impact on your stress levels. If you already have an inherited low stress tolerance, as we discussed in Chapter Two, a score of even 150 can lead to you being over stressed. However, for the majority with average stress tolerance a score of more than 250 is a potential red flag. It indicates that we are over stressed and need to start thinking about what action we can take to reduce that score as much as we can.

When to See Your Doctor

Initially there are many practical self-help methods we can use to start addressing our stress levels and we will look at those shortly.

However, if your stress rating is high and you are experiencing physical symptoms, severe distress or having difficulty functioning normally, then it is advisable to see your doctor sooner rather than later and have a thorough check-up. Your doctor will certainly want to see you if you have not been sleeping properly for more than three or four days and you feel permanently tired and exhausted. If your mood is changeable and you are losing your temper more often, or feeling low and depressed, then do not hesitate to get medical help.

Chapter Five

How Your Doctor Can Help

One of the ways in which we often try to cope with stress is almost to push it to the back of our minds and think it will get better by itself. It may do, but it is important to remember that although some stress is a normal part of life, if it goes on for some time then that can lead to other illnesses which will need treatment. Stress has been linked to the development of high blood pressure and heart disease, as well as insomnia and depression, so if you are persistently suffering from any of the following conditions please consult with your doctor:

- fatigue
- aches and pains
- anxiety
- problems with sleeping
- lack of enjoyment of life.

Stress is so multi-faceted that there is no single test that will help your doctor to diagnose what is wrong, but they will be able to assess you from the physical and emotional symptoms that you display. They may also want to do certain tests to establish if there are any physical underlying problems that might be causing your condition. Stress that does not clear up by itself may indicate to your doctor that there a possibility of some other hidden factor, and they will look for any warning signs of diseases such as:

- thyroid disease
- calcium imbalance
- anaemia
- diabetes
- Bi-polar disorder (this is the name now given to the condition that used to be known as manic depression. It is the state in which a person is subject to very exaggerated mood swings, with peaks of elation or mania alternating with troughs of depression).

- liver disease
- kidney malfunction
- vitamin deficiency
- hormone deficiency.

It is possible to have these conditions without being aware of them, but they are potential stressors for your body so your doctor will want to eliminate them as a possible cause.

Your doctor's examination may include a complete physical examination, blood and urine tests, measuring your thyroid and kidney function, levels of your liver enzymes, calcium, phosphorus, iron and blood sugar and a complete blood count.

What about Medication?

When you initially talk with your doctor, he or she is not likely to prescribe medication as the first way to help you cope with stress specifically, although some types of anxiety can be treated with antidepressants. People tend think that tranquillizers such as diazepam (Valium) or temazepam will help, but they are not suitable for treating stress because they can cause addiction after only a few weeks of taking them.

Rather than relying on medicine, it is usually far better to try to identify the things in your life that are causing stress and try to deal with them by other means.

What your doctor will do, having examined you and found out what is causing your stress or what condition you are exhibiting as a result of stress, is to start off with some self-help measures. Usually they suggest tackling your lifestyle and examining factors such your diet, exercise or lack of it, alcohol consumption and whether you smoke. Once your doctor has done the initial assessment, they may also prescribe drugs to help with specific symptoms that you are currently exhibiting and that are associated with stress.

Do please bear in mind that all prescribing is individual and none of these suggestions is to be taken as an indicator of what your doctor should prescribe for you. They represent only what is available and what they may use their judgement to decide would be the best regime for you. If we look at some of the more common conditions associated with high stress levels we can see what other help your doctor can offer.

Anxiety

There are a number of anti-anxiety drugs that work to reduce persistent feelings of nervousness and tension, but they are only a short-term measure and in addition to medication your doctor will probably suggest tackling the root cause of the anxiety through other methods, such as hypnotherapy or counselling. The physical symptoms of anxiety are produced by an increase in the activity of the sympathetic nervous system when the chemical brain transmitter noradrenaline (our 'fight or flight' stimulant) is released. Two main groups of drugs are used: beta blockers and benzodiazepines.

Beta blockers are generally prescribed for reducing physical symptoms such as palpitations or shaking when faced with specific stress like interviews or public speaking. As their name suggests, beta blockers block the action of noradrenaline in the body and so reduce the symptoms.

More widely used are the benzodiazepines, and these work by reducing feelings of agitation and restlessness. In essence they slow the body and brain down and can produce feelings of drowsiness, and you may feel less motivated or more apathetic than normal. Although considered safe in small doses over the short term, these drugs can produce psychological and physical dependence and for this reason are normally prescribed for periods of two weeks or less. If taken for longer, they need to be reduced gradually under medical supervision as stopping suddenly can lead to withdrawal symptoms.

Depression

Weepiness, apathy and changes of mood are often associated with stress, but if a prolonged period of sadness or indifference to life goes on then your doctor may consider anti-depressant drugs. As we saw in Chapter Two, the chemical balance in our brain is vital in maintaining our mental health and resilience. Generally our brain cells release enough of the 'positive' chemical messengers to stimulate the other cells in the brain, but it is believed that depression occurs when these positive messengers become overwhelmed and unable to maintain their normal function. The purpose of antidepressants is to increase the level of these positive neurotransmitters to redress the balance and to change the mood. Three types of drug are generally used: tricyclics, monoamine oxidase inhibitors (MOAs), and serotonin re-uptake inhibitors (SRIs).

Tricyclics are often the first group of drugs to be prescribed and fall into two categories; those such as amitriptyline, which are sedative in nature, and others like imipramine, which are excitatory and helpful for lethargy and apathy. MOAs are effective if you are suffering from anxiety or phobias as well as depression, or do not respond well to tricyclics. SRIs raise the levels of serotonin available to the brain and, as we have previously seen, good levels of serotonin are essential to regulate sleep and mood.

Antidepressants do not normally start to take effect for at least 10 to 14 days and it can be up to 6 to 8 weeks before the full benefit is felt. Side effects with this group of drugs can be unpleasant and vary a great deal from individual to individual, so your doctor may want to adjust or change your medication several times and it can take a while to find the exact drug and dose that will work best for you.

Digestive Upsets and Inflammatory Bowel Disease

It is the job of our digestive system to change the food that comes into our body as protein, fat or carbohydrate into the simpler molecules that the body can use. Our digestive system consists of the mouth, oesophagus, duodenum, small and large intestines, colon, rectum and anus and problems can manifest in any of these areas.

Stress is often reflected in a breakdown of our normal digestive processes, so we may experience symptoms from simple indigestion and constipation to more serious illnesses such as Crohn's disease, which is an inflammation of the bowel, and ulcerative colitis, where the large intestine becomes inflamed.

Your doctor might suggest antacids for ulcers and excess stomach acid or simple bulking agents to help with constipation. They will also probably want you to keep a record of your diet so that you can analyse if there are particular foods, or combinations of foods, that are upsetting you. The more serious conditions of the digestive system, like Crohn's disease, are definitely linked with high levels of stress and this may be something your doctor will want you to address immediately as well as prescribing the relevant drugs for your condition.

Fatigue and Exhaustion
Continuously feeling tired and exhausted as a result of stress is something that will probably not be addressed immediately with medication, but your doctor will want to investigate to find out what is causing it. Under stress we are not always able to absorb the full range of nutrients in our food, or we may be skipping meals so that our diet becomes unbalanced, and your doctor may surprise you by suggesting or prescribing nutritional supplements or a tonic to boost your immune system.

High Blood Pressure
Raised blood pressure is a very common symptom of stress and if lifestyle changes do not bring it down to normal levels, or you have a family history of heart disease or strokes, then your doctor may want to try medication to control it. Certain groups of people are more at risk from continuous high blood pressure; diabetics, those with high cholesterol levels, and smokers. A first stage is often to try diuretics to increase the body's excretion of water from the bloodstream via the kidneys. By doing this the total volume of blood circulating through the body is reduced and this reduces the pressure in the blood vessels. If that is not effective the next stage might be vasodilators to improve blood flow by expanding the diameter of the blood vessels. Other drug groups that can be used, depending on your personal circumstances, are digitalis drugs, beta blockers, anti-arrhythmics, anti-angina drugs, antihypertensives, lipid-lowering drugs and drugs that affect how the blood clots.

Low Stress Tolerance
As we have seen, some people definitely have a lower ability to cope with stress; the stress test in Chapter Four will have given you an idea of whether this relates to you or not, and you may need to take additional action to help you get back to normal. We know that if that if we are not getting the right balance of positive and negative brain messages to keep us in balance, then that can lead to stress-related problems, particularly relating to mood. If you have lowered

your stress levels as much as you can, and if you have no hidden physical illness that is adding hidden stress to your life, and you are still stressed then you could one of those people whose predisposition or genetic inheritance does not allow you to make enough positive chemical messengers to handle your daily stress load.

If you are someone who is unusually susceptible to stress, then your doctor might suggest a short course of a group of drugs that work by rebalancing your brain's chemical messages to alter the positive and negative balance and help you cope better. There are two general categories of such drugs: tricyclics, which boost serotonin, dopamine and noradrenaline; and the selective serotonin reuptake inhibitors, or SSRIs, which act mainly to boost serotonin function. Both groups are equally effective, and which ones your doctor prescribes will depend mainly on what symptoms of stress you are having.

Migraines

Migraine headaches are caused by changes in the blood vessels and stress is certainly one of the triggers. This is due to the way in which our blood pressure rises when we are stressed, and the effect of serotonin in causing the large blood vessels in the brain to constrict, so there is a double pressure on the blood flow to the brain.

Treatment is given to either prevent attacks or to relieve symptoms such as nausea, flashing lights, vomiting or numbness and tingling in the arms. The type of attacks you are prone to will decide what type of drugs you may be given, but preventive drugs include the antidepressant amitriptyline, clonidine, methysergide, pizotifen and propranolol. Symptomatic relief drugs include over-the-counter medications like aspirin, codeine and paracetamol and prescription drugs like ergotamine and sumatriptan.

Sleeping Problems

Nowadays doctors are reluctant to prescribe sleeping tablets until other self-help remedies have been tried or until they can see that lack of sleep is clearly adversely affecting your overall health. Drugs for sleeping disorders depress brain function by interfering with the chemical activity in the brain and nervous system. This reduces communication between the cells — literally by reducing the 'chatter' that goes on — and this allows you to fall asleep more easily.

However, for restful sleep we need to have the full range from light sleep, deep sleep and dream sleep, which is the normal pattern. Unfortunately sleeping drugs interfere with this pattern because while depressing overall brain function they also suppress our dream state sleep and this can leave us feeling heavy and as if we have not had a really restful night's sleep. Many people also find that they can feel the effects of the drug well into the next day, so normal alertness and focus are diminished.

Although drugs to relieve poor sleep habits can be highly effective initially, their impact diminishes after the first few nights and again are usually only prescribed for short-term use.

You and Your Doctor

Whatever medication your doctor decides to prescribe, remember that working to reduce stress is a partnership between the two of you. Drugs alone will not effectively give you long-term relief from your symptoms; you will also need to address the underlying causes and take action to reduce or eradicate them.

Chapter Six

Self-help Options

It is clear that stress is an integral and essential part of our daily lives. For life to be enjoyable we all need challenges that are manageable, but there are times when we simply cannot cope and we become stressed and overwhelmed. This is not a sign of weakness, but a perfectly normal response to the sometimes overwhelming change and strain of daily life. What seems to make a major difference is the attitude that you approach the stress with, and the help you are prepared to ask for from others and the support you are willing to accept.

We are never going to be able to entirely eliminate stress from our lives, and so it makes sense to learn how to manage it effectively so we that are less overwhelmed by it. People react differently to the situations they have to face because we are all unique individuals. Your response to life may be easy-going and reflective, or dynamic and competitive, or something in between. Your personality will affect how you deal with the stress in your life, and to some extent how much of it you may attract. Because all our life experiences and conditioning do vary enormously, so too will our response to stress and the degree to which it will affect our overall good health.

Life today is certainly faster-paced and more complex and we are having to adjust continually to rapid change in all areas, particularly those involving technology. As we have seen, change is one of the elements that can produce stress and so we need to develop some strong coping strategies so that we are more resilient to those pressures.

Our more traditional responses of trying to prod ourselves into more life with stimulants such as alcohol, overeating the wrong foods, caffeine and smoking will help us only in the short term. What we are looking for are ways to help us make positive lifestyle changes that will improve our health and help us cope better in the long term. It is very important to take positive action when faced with stress as, if experienced over a period of time, it can seriously impair your mental and physical health.

What it is very heartening to know is that stress is one of the conditions that responds positively to many simple self-help measures. Indeed, as we have seen, it will be the first suggestion that your doctor may make in order to start reducing or eliminating the stresses you are under. The first step is to try to identify the areas in your life that are causing you stress, and the simple questionnaire in Chapter Four may have helped you begin to do that. Although it isn't always possible either to change or to avoid the things that stress you, there are some very simple lifestyle changes that can make all the difference. All of the suggestions here are for you to consider and you can try one, or several, of them for yourself to see what effect they might have on reducing your stress levels.

The Basic Rules

There are three very important rules in successfully employing any self-help methods for stress reduction:

1   Learn to read your own body so that you are aware of the physical signs of stress and what changes take place. Be aware of your own warning signs – this could be a sudden feeling of anxiety, extreme tiredness, feeling very tearful, catching every cough and cold or feeling run down. Use a diary or notebook to record your thoughts and feelings so that you have a record to refer back to and use as a guide.

2   It is not possible to keep adding to your stress load without severe consequences for your health, so investigate whether you can do an exchange. This means that if a new stress has come into your life you need to look for ways in which you could exchange that new stress for one you currently have. It's about eliminating one source of stress so that you don't get overloaded. For example, if your job has suddenly become much more demanding and you have started to plan major renovation or redecoration at home, then put that on hold while you deal with the stress at work.

3   Begin to explore and then develop a 'tool box' of techniques you can call on in different situations. There is no one single thing that will solve all your stress problems because they may well

be different. For instance, getting stressed in a traffic jam will need different techniques from the stress caused by planning a large function or public speaking.

In order to put those rules into operation, think of stress reduction as having five main areas to work on: stress management, diet, lifestyle, exercise and relaxation. You don't have to look at them all immediately; try one or more areas at a time so you don't add to your stress by trying to do everything at once! We will look at these areas in detail in the following chapters, and in addition to self-help methods there are also many alternative therapies that can be useful and you will find information on those in Chapter Twelve. But, first, listed below are a few tips to get you started before going into the individual elements of a self-help programme.

Instant Help

There are times when we need something quick and instant that will reduce the stress we are feeling. Here are a few tips that can help us feel calmer and relieve some of our tension:

- Take some deep calming breaths, in the open air if you can, or at least by an open window. If you normally breathe quickly or shallowly, then count as you breathe in for a count of six, hold it for a count of three and then breathe out again for a count of six to really empty your lungs and get rid of any stale air. Even three or four good breaths will bring in plenty of oxygen to help revitalize your cells.
- Another breathing technique that only takes a minute is called alternate nostril breathing and it comes from the practice of yoga. It's an instant way to feel calmer and once you have done it once or twice it will feel quite natural and comfortable, though you may feel a little awkward at first. Begin by placing your right thumb lightly on your right nostril and breathing in deeply through your left nostril. Close your left nostril with your middle finger as you release your right thumb and exhale through your right nostril. Now breathe in deeply through the right nostril, and exhale through the left. This is one complete cycle, and just

49

continue to do this until you feel more relaxed.

- If everything is getting on top of you, sit quietly at your desk or table and give yourself a minute's break by doing an exercise called palming. Rest your elbows on the table, softly fold your hands into a cup shape, bend your head forward, close your eyes and place your hands over your eye sockets to completely cover them. You may feel slight pressure on your brow or cheek bone, but just allow yourself to relax and block out the world for a short time. It is also very helpful if you have been working for long periods on a computer, or doing close work and feel your eyes are strained or tired.

- Call a friend and have a chat; even five minutes will help release some of your stress and take you out of your own concerns.

- If you are feeling tense, then essential oil of lavender is very calming and relaxing. Either put it directly under your nose and sniff it straight from the bottle, or put just a few drops on a handkerchief or tissue and inhale slowly. If you have more time, run a warm, relaxing bath and add the lavender oil to that.

- When you are feeling panicky or fearful, then a flower remedy such as Bach Rescue Remedy will help restore emotional balance. Just put seven drops under your tongue for immediate relief.

- Yawn, hugely and widely, so that you get rid of the tension in your jaw and allow in even more life-giving oxygen.

- Talking through what is concerning you with a friend, partner or even a professional can help reduce the stress because speaking of your feelings is a very good way of reducing the internal pressure you experience if you are bottling everything up. A word of caution here. If your major cause of stress is someone else's behaviour, take care how you approach them. A spirit of co-operation to share what the problem is can be very helpful, but make sure they don't feel blamed or accused. It might make you feel temporarily better, but the long-term solution lies in working with others for greater understanding, and blame and anger don't produce that effect.

- Smile: it will release tension in the face, where we carry quite a lot, and will make you look much less stressed. If you think of something positive that genuinely gives you pleasure you will also be helping to lift your mood.

Chapter Seven

Diet and Nutrition

The most fundamental aspect of staying well is to eat and drink those things that support your body and do not stress it. To keep you healthy, and your stress levels down, you need to have an adequate diet that supplies all the nutritional needs that your body and mind demand. Unfortunately when we are stressed, we tend to turn to those things that give us an instant lift or are not necessarily that healthy but make us feel good. Eating for comfort is natural when we are under pressure, but there are foods that help and those that will hinder your effectively coping with stress. We will look at what makes an ideal diet to tackle stress shortly, but the simplest way to start looking at the connection between your diet and the stress you are under is to keep a food and mood diary for at least a week.

Any simple notebook will do. Write down everything you eat, including drinks and snacks, and then also note any physical or emotional changes you notice shortly afterwards. The notes can be as short or long as you like: this record is just for you, and you will find that the more detail you put down the better your chance of identifying food problem areas or even hidden allergies that you are not currently aware of. This is an example of how it might look:

FOOD AND MOOD DIARY

	Monday
8.00 a.m.	Coffee and cigarette. Woke me up, but felt dizzy shortly afterwards.
10.30 a.m.	Can of cola and Danish pastry at work. Was feeling tired, but gave me a lift. Felt tired again by 11.30 a.m.
1.00 p.m.	Hamburger and chips for lunch, and another cola. Felt bloated and a bit sick. Ate a chocolate bar on the way back to the office, felt a bit edgy.
3.00 p.m	Tea and a cigarette. Felt tired after lunch and this picked me up. Irritable on the phone with a customer.

6.00 p.m.   Beer in the pub then a Chinese meal. Noticed a bit of
                   tingling in my hands after the meal.

You can see that it helps to be as specific as possible so that you can
link foods and emotional/physical states. Rather than 'a chocolate
bar' say what it was, and exactly what you ate and drank for that
Chinese meal. You might notice that drinking too much coffee or
cola can makes you shake and increases your irritability or mood
swings and so you can think about cutting down or switching to
something that doesn't jangle your nerves.

A number of people are sensitive to monosodium glutamate,
which is used in many Chinese restaurants and ready-prepared
meals, so if you notice after-effects from such food you could again
think about switching to another dish from the menu that doesn't
contain it, or avoid it for a while as you are more likely to be
sensitive to it when under stress. If you feel you might be sensitive
to specific foods, or allergic to certain substances, then signs to look
for are things like wheezing, a stuffy or runny nose, a skin rash of any
kind and a loosening of bowel movements, or even diarrhoea. These
could be signs of an allergic reaction so you might want to avoid that
item for a while and not subject your body to the extra stress of
dealing with something that is an irritant to it.

You are not looking to necessarily immediately change your diet,
but to be aware of what you are really eating and what the patterns
are. Often we eat unconsciously, grabbing a snack here or there and
'forgetting' about the odd doughnut or bag of crisps. To see it written
down in black and white might seem a bit daunting, but it will make
you aware of whether you are nurturing or depleting your body,
which is what we will look at next.

Stress Preventers

Water

For an immediate reduction in stress just start to drink more water, as
a dehydrated system can lead to feelings of anxiety because your
body is constantly checking on whether it has sufficient supplies to
carry out all its normal activities. If you have a low fluid intake there
may be only just enough to maintain essential bodily services, and

water has to be diverted away from what are seen as non-essential areas, like the skin. That's why one of the signs of dehydration is dry, tight or flaking skin, so rather than putting on a face cream to correct it you could try drinking more water first to see if that helps.

Many foods do already contain water in varying proportions, but your body needs a constant supply of fluid and that doesn't include coffee, tea and alcohol. Plain, non-carbonated water is what your body wants because every one of your physical functions relies on it. Whether it's needed for the elimination of waste and toxins from the bowel or to regulate your body temperature, you can help things run more smoothly by drinking at least six to eight glasses a day. It is best taken between meals as drinking a lot with your food it can interfere with digestion by diluting your gastric juices.

Starting the day with a glass of warm water will help in two ways: first, it replenishes the dehydration that takes place overnight as your body has used up its stores in the regular cellular renewal and repair work that is continually going on; and, second, it will help move the bowel and prevent constipation, which can be another symptom of stress.

If you are not used to drinking water just for its own sake, then start off by having a glass of water before you have a cup of tea or coffee so you are automatically doubling your fluid intake. Or you could place a 1.5 or 2 litre bottle of water on your desk or in the kitchen next to the kettle and keep topping up your glass. It can be hard to keep track of how many glasses a day you are having, but if you aim to drink the whole bottle over the course of a day you can see exactly how much you have had, or how little.

Carbohydrate

Both the brain and the nervous system require glucose, and that comes from the unrefined sugars found in carbohydrates. Our brains use up more of our carbohydrate stores (around 40 per cent) than any other part of the body, and when you are stressed the brain is often in overdrive from being constantly preoccupied with worry, anxiety or fear. Keen concentration and focus also draws upon the carbohydrate supplies it needs to keep you alert, so if your diet is low in this essential ingredient you may experience symptoms such as dizziness, digestive upsets, fatigue, insomnia, poor concentration, irritability or weepiness.

Carbohydrates also enhance your brain's uptake of the amino acid tryptophan, which the brain then converts into serotonin, so these foods will make you feel calmer and more relaxed. Their effect lasts in the body for roughly three hours; that is why it is good advice to eat little and often, so that you keep the serotonin levels stable.

Because carbohydrates release their glucose into the body slowly over a long period they have a balancing effect, and can stabilize both energy levels and moods. If you eat plenty of carbohydrate on a regular basis you will help reduce your stress levels, but not all carbohydrates have the same positive effect.

There are basically two types of carbohydrate: simple and complex. It is the slow-releasing complex carbohydrates that are most beneficial to us for stabilizing mood. We think of them as the 'healthy' foods that are generally included in most ideal diets and consist of the wholegrains found in cereals, brown rice, grains, bread and pasta, vegetables, beans and pulses. We will look at the less beneficial carbohydrates in the next section, but you should aim to have at least 60 per cent of your daily intake coming from complex carbohydrates to keep you in balance.

As well as eating more wholegrains, try to eat fresh vegetables and salad because they help to increase the brain's serotonin production, and the more of those positive messengers you are producing, the better your emotional balance and moods.

Fruit is a simple carbohydrate because it principally consists of fructose which enters the bloodstream fairly quickly, unlike the complex carbohydrates which take time to be broken down, and it is the process of converting that fructose into glucose in the body that will release energy. If you are feeling fatigued and tired, then snacking on fresh fruit will give you a boost that is longer-lasting and more beneficial than a chocolate bar. Some fruits are quicker to enter the bloodstream than others; athletes are great fans of bananas because they act quickly to raise blood sugar levels – very valuable if you are running out of your natural energy reserves.

Fresh fruit and vegetables provide us with a wide range of nutrients, vitamins, fluid and fibre as well as replenishing our energy stores, so it makes sense to have at least the recommended five portions a day. The British favourite, the potato, can form the basis of a great stress-busting meal if you combine it with salad and some protein for maximum nutritional effect.

Protein

Protein needs to form at least 10–15 per cent of our daily diet and also helps balance blood sugar. If you combine it with your complex carbohydrates, then they seem to act together to slow down the energy release of the carbohydrate, thus making it available to the body for longer. Protein need not just be meat-or fish-based; milk, eggs, cheese, pulses and beans are also good sources.

Combining protein with carbohydrates also helps improve uptake of serotonin, and this is generally how most of our meals are put together so it is more a case of getting the balance right between the greater amount of carbohydrate to protein. Because traditionally protein foods have been more expensive, like meat for example, we have eaten less of it as a part of a meal. However, modern production methods have drastically reduced the cost of meat protein and we eat far more of it, and far more often, than we would have done in the past. This is not the healthiest balance to reduce stress: remember you want to have 60 per cent carbohydrate to 10–15 per cent of protein, not the other way round. Examples of protein and carbohydrate foods are baked beans on wholemeal toast or chicken and rice, meat and potatoes, fish and chips.

If one of your stress symptoms is not being able to think clearly or to focus, then make sure you are getting your daily minimum amount of protein because it really can make a difference. It stimulates your brain to produce dopamine and norepinephrine, two chemicals that keep you attentive and alert.

Because it takes roughly four hours for your body to break down protein, try to allocate it so that you have enough protein at breakfast and lunch to carry you through the day and then concentrate on carbohydrates in the evening to help you relax and unwind. If you are starting to lose concentration mid-afternoon, you can add in some more protein from having a glass of milk, rather than a cup of coffee.

Stress Promoters

Refined Carbohydrates

Refined carbohydrates don't release their energy slowly over a sustained period of time like the complex carbohydrates, but act much more quickly so that your blood sugar levels are pushed up very fast. Initially this can feel good as we get an instant hit of energy, but that rapid rise is followed by an equally rapid fall in the blood sugar levels and we are back to feeling tired or anxious again. This is a cycle that can be hard to break because our instinct when the blood sugar levels fall is to try to replace them again so we have another 'quick fix' snack and on we go again.

Refined carbohydrates are often what we think of as 'treats': cakes, biscuits, non-wholegrain cereals and sweets. They are made from flour that has been processed and refined so that the wholegrain element has been lost, and they usually contain high amounts of both fat and sugar. Of course they are fine in moderation, but when we are stressed we tend to comfort eat or artificially try to boost our mood or energy levels and these products are indeed a very readily available and fast way to do that. However, there are other ways of lifting energy from snack sources that won't have this yo-yo effect and you will find them listed later in this chapter.

Sugar

Erratic mood swings, less capacity to concentrate and energy levels that resemble a rollercoaster are some of the problems associated with sugar. We are familiar with its effects on hyperactivity and agitation in children, and there is no reason to think that as adults our bodies respond any differently. Research has implicated high sugar consumption in aggressive behaviour, depression, anxiety and fatigue. These are also common symptoms of stress, and eating lots of sugar in your diet can make your stress levels worse.

Sugar is actually of very little nutritional value. It depletes our body of essential vitamins and minerals needed to deal with stress, but actually gives us very little in return except for lots of calories. The sugar that you add to drinks or foods is visible, and you may feel that you don't have a sugar problem, but there are so many hidden sugars in everyday items from toothpaste to patent medicines and condiments like tomato ketchup that it is easy to be taking it unawares. If you can, reduce your intake and start to check labels to see where the hidden sugars are, and if you can manage to give up sugar entirely for a while you will soon see how it is affecting your mood and energy levels.

One tip if you really feel you can't manage without a quick sugar hit when you are stressed is to combine it with some protein and fat. The sugar only has a stimulant effect for around an hour in your body, and if you put in more it can overload the system and you will feel drained and sluggish. Combine a sugary snack with some protein and fat, say from a glass of milk, and it will help to balance out the sugar crash. Ideally, cut out the sugar altogether, but if you feel you really can't give it up, then this might just help in the short term.

A word of caution about substituting sweeteners for sugar. Artificial sweeteners can have several adverse effects on the body that are particularly relevant to those who are stressed. Some appear to trigger the stress response in the brain and if used long-term may also adversely affect serotonin levels which may also have an effect on increasing symptoms of depression. Other side effects in those using sweeteners long-term can include digestive upsets and diarrhoea, so to reduce the impact of stress on your body it would be sensible to reduce the use of sweeteners as much as possible.

Stressful Stimulants

If you have to produce a report in double-quick time, or have suddenly got twice as much to do as you had planned for, it is tempting to turn to the quick stimulants to help you through. They are very familiar to us, and the most common are caffeine, chocolate, sugar, alcohol and cigarettes. They all have their different drawbacks, and certain things in common.

What all stimulants do is to increase your levels of the stress hormones adrenaline and cortisol so that you are ready for any 'fight or flight' situation, whether it is a potentially acrimonious meeting with the boss or finishing your increasing long 'to do' list. Physically you are using stimulants to get yourself in a state of readiness, or to feel you have the focus and concentration to deal with the situation. They will increase your heart rate temporarily, but afterwards you can feel agitated, restless, jittery and even more stressed.

Caffeine

Caffeine has a particularly strong effect on our system and is found in coffee, colas, tea, chocolate and many of the newly-popular 'energy drinks'. It has not just one, but three different stimulants – caffeine, theobromine and theophylline – and they raise blood pressure, stimulate the heart and also desensitize the body to its own naturally produced dopamine and adrenaline. This last effect is directly increased in relation to the amount of caffeine you are taking in, and leads to the body's natural ability to regulate itself being overwhelmed. Up to two cups a day seems to be fine for most people, unless you have a particular sensitivity to it, and they are best drunk in the morning or early afternoon. The highly stimulant nature of caffeine interferes with your ability to change to the slower, more relaxed physical state you need to be in so that you are ready and prepared for a good night's sleep. If you are having sleeping problems it would be advisable not to have coffee, or hot chocolate which also is high in caffeine, much later than 6.00 or 7.00 p.m.

If you think you must be all right because you never drink coffee, you could still be in just as much danger of caffeine overload. If you can't get through the day without several strong cups of tea, you might be surprised to learn that each one of them contains as much caffeine as a weak cup of coffee. If you love sugary, carbonated colas and energy drinks, then have a look at the list of ingredients on the side of the can. They will usually contain between 45 mg and 80 mg of caffeine, and that's the same amount you would get from an average cup of coffee.

Chocolate has both caffeine and theobromine, but if you must eat it, go for plain, dark chocolate as it encourages a greater production of feel-good tryptophan than does white or milk chocolate.

If you are not sure whether you are having too much caffeine, the side effects can include agitation, panic attacks, palpitations and migraines.

Social Stimulants

Tobacco and alcohol use often seem to go together and although the general reason for smoking and drinking is often to feel more relaxed, the actual end result is anything but.

Tobacco
Tobacco can affect the ability of the coronary arteries to respond to stress. A study found that smokers, on average, had about 14 per cent less blood flow to the heart compared to non-smokers. Tobacco contains nicotine, which initially does have a soothing effect on the nerves or can make you feel more alert, depending on your mood. Unfortunately you also get withdrawal effects immediately you finish each cigarette. These include irritability and poor concentration, and because smoking also suppresses the appetite, your chances of maintaining good nutrition to support your body during stressful periods is also reduced. Excess stomach acid is produced when you smoke, and if your stress shows in your stomach with heartburn or wind, then it would be a sensible precaution to reduce or cut out tobacco to avoid those particular symptoms. The general health risks associated with smoking are well known and severe, from terminal cancers to heart disease, and it is highly addictive.

Alcohol
Unlike tobacco, alcohol in moderation can have some positive health benefits for managing stress. A glass of red wine for instance will relax us and its antioxidants have some positive effects on our heart and circulatory system. The key here is moderation because in excess it can make the symptoms of stress worse and it is often used to hide from or avoid the actual causes of the stress. In particular it can make aggressive behaviour and violent mood swings worse and affect our ability to think clearly or focus properly. There is also the fact that alcohol depresses our positive brain messenger function and makes us more liable to feel emotionally vulnerable, weepy or depressed. Some people may turn to alcohol to help them sleep, and again initially it may do so, but the effect of alcohol on the brain means that you are not getting a true sleep and do not wake feeling refreshed – in fact, the opposite is usually the case.

Allergies and Additives
Anything that makes your body have to work harder than it needs to will be stressful. Being allergic to certain foods means your body will do its best either to absorb or expel it, and both those actions take energy that you may not have to spare when you are under

stress. The body's forced response to what it sees as 'foreign' substances from either allergies or additives will also affect your brain messenger function, and so may have a noticeable effect on your moods. Food allergies are sadly common these days, and your food and mood diary may give you some clues as to where your particular sensitivities lie.

Nutritionists usually say that the most common allergic substances in the developed world are sugar, caffeine, wheat and dairy products. If you suspect you have a problem with any of these, then the simplest way to test it is to remove that item from your diet for at least two weeks and see if you notice any difference. If you think you have more than one allergic reaction to different foods, or specific products, only eliminate one at a time. This way you can have an accurate picture of your response to that particular food or substance, whereas if you try eliminating several at once you will not know for sure which of them, or which ones, are the real problem. Very accurate reporting in your food and mood diary will also help you pinpoint whether it is, say, all cola drinks that are a problem or just the supermarket's own brand that you have recently started buying.

If you do eliminate a potential problem, like coffee, then you may experience some of the symptoms of withdrawal. We may not think of ourselves as addicted to everyday items like sugar, wheat or chocolate but the acid test is when you cut them out of your daily diet. You may notice that you are desperate for, or crave, the missing item and also have symptoms like headaches, nausea or dizziness. It can seem that the more we like something, the more probable that we are either allergic or addicted to it and stopping for two weeks will let you know where your problem areas with food lie. If you are getting withdrawal symptoms, then increase the amount of water you are drinking as that will help flush the toxins and allergic substance out of your body faster.

Food additives such as some of the E number colours and flavours do adversely affect some people, particularly children, and a widely-used additive to ready prepared and restaurant meals is monosodium glutamate. Its function is to enhance the flavour of the food, but unfortunately it can also have a number of side effects in sensitive people ranging from tingling in the hands to anxiety or extreme nervousness.

Nor does an additive have to be unnatural to have an effect on you. Salt is the most common condiment that we use, but it can be harmful in certain cases. It should be used in moderation, especially by those with high blood pressure, and too liberal a use on food can also lead to feelings of tension. You can be allergic to anything, including things like fruit or vegetables that you might think would be healthy, such as garlic or strawberries for instance. We each react individually, and in different degrees, and undoubtedly stress makes our body more sensitive to potential irritants so something you have never had a problem with may become so when you are under extreme stress.

The Anti-stress Diet

When we feel stressed, the first thing we tend to do is reach for immediate fixes in the form of high-fat and sugar-filled foods. As we have seen, however, indulging in these kinds of comfort foods will not do you any favours in the long run and can add to your stress levels rather than reduce them. We all have particular preferences as to the kind of food we like to eat, and how we like to cook it, and there is no need to drastically alter your diet overnight, but you might find it helpful to incorporate some of these ideas to see if they make a positive difference to your stress levels.

When you are anxious and stressed it is important to make sure that what you eat is not contributing to your panicky state. This diet concentrates on fruit, vegetables and wholegrain foods to provide a good base of complex carbohydrates which will increase the amount of serotonin in your brain. This tranquillizing effect will help you cope with everyday pressure and anxiety much more easily. The objective is to keep your blood sugar levels even and avoid the great fluctuations that can occur when we use sugar or other stimulants to try to balance our moods.

Whatever you plan to eat, make sure you never skip meals, and if you can, try to have smaller meals more often, rather than two or three main meals a day. Your body will find it much easier to cope if you can do this. If stress has affected your appetite or your digestion, then consider having more of your food in liquid form, such as soups, fruit smoothies or vegetable juices, as these will provide you with good nutrition that is easy for the body to absorb. If you have a blender or juicer, then it can be a great ally in providing nutritious food that is easy to digest.

Stress Reducers Reminder List

Here is a quick checklist to help you put together a daily menu that will incorporate the things that will genuinely help you reduce stress.

- Lots of water to prevent dehydration.
- Complex carbohydrates like brown rice and potatoes, wholegrain products like bread, pasta and cereals.
- Protein to stimulate dopamine production and give us more focus and concentration. Best from fish, turkey, chicken and pulses when combined with complex carbohydrates.
- Turkey and milk are both good sources of tryptophan – a precursor of seratonin – so include them if you need more calming foods.
- Fresh fruit, especially bananas which are a good source of tryptophan, your natural antidepressant.
- Fruit and vegetable juices, focusing on those which are red, dark green, yellow and orange in colour as they are higher in the antioxidants that help protect the heart.
- Vitamin C-rich foods including oranges, lemons, grapefruit, lime, kiwi fruit, strawberries, blackcurrants, melon, red, yellow and orange peppers, green vegetables like broccoli and mangetout peas.
- Dairy foods, lettuce, oranges and avocados may not have much in common except they all contain bromine which helps us relax.
- Foods that are rich in vitamin B support the nervous system and defend it from stress. These include dairy foods, brewer's yeast, wholegrains, liver, lentils, seafood and dark green leafy vegetables.
- Zinc-rich foods keep our immune system healthy, found in shellfish, liver, lamb, beef wheatgerm, seeds, nuts and tofu.
- Calming calcium foods including dairy produce, soya milk and yoghurt, pulses, nuts, seeds, tinned salmon, tuna and mackerel.
- Magnesium-rich foods like barley, bulgar wheat, brown rice and lentils.

- Increase the fibre in your diet and you will reduce the risk of heart disease as fibre absorbs cholesterol in your blood. Fibre-rich foods include bananas, potatoes with the skin left on, wholemeal breads and pasta, unsalted nuts, dried fruit, brown rice, beans and pulses.
- A good variety of vegetables to maintain good levels of vitamins and minerals. Fresh if possible, but good frozen vegetables can have more nutrients than those that have been sitting on the greengrocer's shelf for a while. Frozen peas in particular are an excellent source of both vitamin C and fibre.
- The body needs time to digest food properly, and eating too close to bedtime does put a strain on your digestive system. To make it easy on yourself always allow at least three hours after eating before going to bed.

Stress Aggravator Reminder List

It isn't always possible to avoid everything on the list, but these are some guidelines for things you should avoid where possible, and certainly cut out if you can.

- Refined foods and snacks like cakes, biscuits, carbonated drinks, sweets and chocolate. They will unbalance your blood sugar levels and leave you more tired and stressed. Replace them with wholemeal flour products and sweeten with honey or fruit spreads.
- Sugar in all its forms, including sweets and chocolate, and artificial sweeteners.
- Check the labels of all products you buy to avoid chemical additives and preservatives where possible, and generally go for the minimum number of ingredients in ready-prepared foods.
- Convenience foods are exactly what they say they are, but are best kept to a minimum. Chilled ready meals are very popular, but too many of them are high in artificial and chemical flavours, colours and preservatives, or added salt, sugars and fats to improve flavour.
- Cigarettes and alcohol, as they will increase stress levels and have associated health risks.

- Coffee, tea, colas and chocolate all contain high levels of caffeine and are best reduced or avoided.
- Reduce saturated fat in your diet to reduce your cholesterol levels and your blood pressure. Saturated fats include those found in red meat, lard, butter and margarine, full-fat milk, cream, mayonnaise, pastries, biscuits, chocolate and crisps.

Daily Food Suggestions

If there is one overwhelming thing that would improve your nutrition, it would be to make your food as natural as possible. Preparing and cooking food can be very relaxing, and you have complete control over what goes in it. Make it easy on yourself by having some of these positive foods in your kitchen, ready to go, so that if you come home tired and depressed you have something to help lift your mood, rather than reaching for another glass of wine or ringing for a take-out meal. Experiment to see what foods you notice have a good result, and keep your food and mood diary up to date for long-term and accurate diet adjustment.

It is sensible to reduce fat, sugar and salt in your daily diet and to reduce the amount of red meat in favour of chicken, turkey and fish as they have positive health benefits for your mood and general well-being. Oily fish in particular, which contain Omega 3 oils, are now believed to help block production of the enzyme that makes us tense under pressure.

Breakfast

Breakfast is the most important meal of the day to get your body replenished and ready to go. Make the time to have a balanced meal here and you will reap the benefits all day. Avoid sugary cereals if you can and focus on getting complex carbohydrate and some protein into your system first thing.

Start with some hot water with a slice of lemon in it, then one of these: wholegrain cereal or muesli with raisins, chopped apple or banana, porridge, wholemeal toast or fruit loaf with cottage cheese, fresh fruit and juice. Add some sunflower, sesame and pumpkin seeds for an even more nutritious breakfast. For protein, go for eggs (poached, scrambled or an omelette), cheese, peanut butter or baked beans.

Have one of your two cups of coffee or tea here if you are not yet ready to give it up, or try a fruit or herbal tea instead.

In a rush? In a blender put a banana or some fresh or frozen raspberries or strawberries, a small pot of live natural or soya yoghurt, and add some protein powder for an instant breakfast that will sustain you right through the morning. Vary the fruit according to the time of year.

Mid-morning Snack
Rather than a cup of coffee or tea, have a glass of milk to help you stay calm and if you are hungry snack on a mixture of nuts (unsalted) and dried or fresh fruit. Walnuts and dates are particularly calming. The 'breakfast' bars that contain grains, nuts and seeds can also be a good standby, but again choose a natural or organic one without artificial additives or high levels of sugar.

Lunch
If you are trying to stay calm, then eat a large salad or keep up the complex carbohydrates with a dish of pasta or a baked potato. If lunch is usually a bought sandwich, go for wholemeal or rye bread and a filling of salad or hummus. If you take your own lunch, have some rye crispbreads and spread with tuna pât[3] or yeast extract. For something more substantial, make up a bowl of pasta with tuna, olive oil and lemon juice and add some vitamin C with chopped yellow, red or orange peppers. Soup is a good healthy alternative, provided it is either home-made or freshly prepared from natural ingredients, and tomato and red peppers are a good de-stressing combination. If, however, you are feeling a bit unfocused and need to be more alert, then have a protein-based lunch like chicken or mackerel with salad or vegetables.

Mid-afternoon Snack
Most of us tend to flag in the middle of the afternoon, so you need something to give you a boost but that won't later drag you down again. Try to avoid tea or coffee, but you could try green tea instead as it can lift your energy and is said to be full of antioxidants that will also boost your immune system. Or go for a fresh vegetable juice like tomato or carrot. Rather than reaching for a biscuit, have an

apple, some grapes or a banana or a handful of brazils, walnuts or almonds as their rich store of essential fatty acids will start to help pick you up.

Dinner
Dinner is the place where you can relax and unwind, so spend some time choosing and cooking food you really like. Try to have oily fish like salmon or mackerel at least once a week as the Omega 3 fatty acids they contain are associated with a lowered incidence of heart disease and that is a risk factor if you are under prolonged stress. Eat a wide range of fresh vegetables, particularly potatoes, both ordinary and sweet potatoes, as they are a great calmer and a good source of vitamin C.

Late-night Snacks
If you have trouble sleeping, try eating a couple of oatcakes with honey half an hour before going to bed. The honey will boost your serotonin levels and help you feel more relaxed and ready to sleep.

If your taste is for savoury rather than sweet, snack on a couple of sticks of celery as it contains a naturally occurring sedative called 3-n-butylphthalide.

Stress-reducing Snacks and Drinks
If you turn to food when you are anxious, instead of going for crisps or sweets, try one of these:

- vegetable sticks with hummus or cottage cheese
- pumpernickel bread with a yeast-based vegetable p†t[3]
- rye crackers or oat cakes with honey
- fruit salad or one piece of any fruit
- natural yoghurt with some honey, maple syrup or dried fruit
- a mixture of half water and half fruit juice instead of carbonated drinks
- camomile tea to soothe the nerves
- peppermint tea to aid digestion or settle a nervy tummy.

Nutritional Supplements

Even if your daily diet is fairly good, at times of stress your body may want some additional help and cause you turn to comfort eating or increase your intake of energy-depleting foods, alcohol or cigarettes. Doctors do now prescribe vitamins for specific conditions and your pharmacy or health store will have a wide range of supplements that specifically target stress. For an individual analysis of what would work best for you it can be helpful to consult a nutritionist, but you could start with just a good basic multivitamin and multi-mineral supplement. If you also feel that you need some extra help, listed below are some of the essential minerals and vitamins that you might want to include in any specific stress-reduction programme. There are of course many more, and if you want to have a comprehensive index of all the nutrients required by your body there are often free or low-priced booklets available with this information in pharmacies and health stores.

B Complex
The top anti-stress supplement is actually a whole series of linked vitamins that together make up what we call the B complex. A deficiency in any one of them will affect your mood and they are all essential for a healthy nervous system. They are responsible for converting the carbohydrates we eat into glucose which the body uses to convert into energy. Our brain uses up the majority of the B vitamins taken into the body and are the first defence against stress. They are not able to be stored, so it is necessary to maintain good regular levels through diet or take a supplement. They are depleted by stress itself, alcohol, coffee and tea. It is not advisable to take B vitamins separately for any length of time without the specific advice of a nutritionist, and it is usually recommended that, for general maintenance, they be taken together in one supplement.

B complex elements include vitamins B1, B3, B5, B6, folic acid and vitamin B12. A deficiency of vitamin B1 can show as physical or mental tiredness and feelings of being unable to concentrate or pay attention because B1 is needed to turn glucose into energy. Vitamin B3, also called niacin, has been used for a number of years to help improve mood and memory and may be suggested for those who are suffering from depression. Vitamin B5, also known as pantothenic acid, is needed to make the neurotransmitter acetylcholine which boosts memory and is also needed to make the stress hormones.

The group of vitamins consisting of B6, B12 and folic acid are vital in the formation of practically all the neurotransmitters in the brain. Together with niacin they control this critical process and deficiency of any one of them can have a serious impact on stress. If you are deficient in B6, for example, you are less able to make serotonin and the positive mood enhancers you need are not available to you, which can increase symptoms of irritability and depression. Stress itself depletes the body, particularly of B6, so it is even more essential to make sure you have adequate amounts to draw on.

If you have feelings of confusion and feel unable to remember things as well as you used to, then it could be a deficiency of B12 that is responsible. It is essential for good mental health as without it the brain simply cannot work properly and serious deficiency of it has been linked to mental health problems such as depression as well as schizophrenia and dementia. Those who follow a strict vegetarian or vegan diet can be at risk of deficiency of this vitamin as it is mainly found in meat, fish, dairy products and eggs and these are normally excluded from such a dietary regime. It is a very simple matter for your doctor to test your blood to see if you are deficient and he or she may then advise you to take a simple supplement, and this will usually be suggested over a very long period, certainly as long as you are on a restricted diet and possibly for the rest of your life. Where there is extreme deficiency or inability to absorb the vitamin properly, it can be administered by injection.

Folic acid, the last component of the B complex, is perhaps best known for being supplemented in pregnancy because it not only protects the baby against conditions like spina bifida, but is also essential for the baby's mental development. If we are deficient in folic acid as adults we may show symptoms of anxiety, irritability, feeling easily tired or depressed.

Vitamin B complex supplements are widely available, and are sometimes also combined with vitamin C for maximum stress busting.

Vitamin C

Our production of adrenaline is reliant on good supplies of vitamin C and because this vitamin is not stored in the body it is rapidly used up when we are under stress. We need it to help balance the neurotransmitters in the brain, to fight infection – to which we can be more susceptible when we are stressed – and it is said to reduce the symptoms of depression. Most of the animal kingdom can make vitamin C in their bodies, but humans cannot and so we must ensure that we have a constant daily amount to supply the body's needs. Because of this, it is advisable to take vitamin C at regular intervals throughout the day, not in one large dose or you will simply excrete through the urine any excess that the body cannot use at that time. It seems that 500 mg doses spread over a day are well tolerated by most people, if you are highly stressed you may want to gradually increase that amount to an overall total of 1 gram to 3 grams taken over several days. If you are taking too much, there are two simple ways that will let you know: you may either get loose bowel movements or diarrhoea, or a tingling sharp sensation on the tongue. In either case, simply stop taking the supplement and when you restart go with a lower dose.

Calcium and Magnesium

Both calcium and magnesium are essential to help relax nerve and muscle cells, and if you have symptoms of anxiety and irritability, or are unable to relax, then you want to make sure you have enough in your diet. The ratio normally suggested is twice the amount of calcium as magnesium and if your diet does not contain much dairy, for calcium, or enough dark green vegetables or nuts, for magnesium, then you might want to consider taking a supplement.

Zinc

If you are feeling demotivated, confused and that your mind is often a complete blank, then zinc deficiency could be one possible reason. If you eat a lot of processed foods, are on a very low-calorie diet or eat very little meat you are likely to have quite low levels of zinc. Aside from its role in maintaining a healthy immune system, it is essential to help the body absorb and fully utilize the stress-busting B complex vitamins.

Last Word

Wherever possible it is good to get your nutritional requirements from food, but if this is not possible then choose a reputable and high-quality range of supplements that contain little, and preferably no, additives, colourings, sugar or sweeteners. If you are in any doubt, do talk to your doctor, pharmacist, nutritionist or health professional to assess what might work best for you.

Chapter Eight

Exercise to Beat Stress

The benefits of exercise are so well known for reducing stress that it is surprising how reluctant we often are to take any. At a conservative estimate you will reduce your risk of premature death by around 40 per cent if you exercise regularly and it is known to help depression, reduce stress and help self-esteem. Starting a gentle, regular exercise routine is one of the first ways easily to start to reduce your stress. If your thoughts about exercise are negative and based around what you did at school then take heart, because there are plenty of ways to exercise that are pleasurable and don't require either special equipment or investment. If you are not a natural fan of going to the gym or taking part in regular sports, don't worry because even the smallest amount of any kind of exercise, even walking round the block, will start to make a difference in helping reduce your stress. There are many benefits to exercise:

1   You will start to burn off any excess adrenaline and other stress hormones that are circulating in your body as a result of that 'fight or flight' response that automatically kicks in when we are stressed. So you are naturally starting to rebalance the stress hormones and get yourself back on an even keel.

2   Exercise increases the amount of oxygen available to the body as you are breathing more deeply. This is of great benefit to your circulatory system as it is then able to transport both nutrients and oxygen more efficiently to all the cells in your body.

3   One of the first things that happens when we are stressed is that the muscles tense up, particularly those in the neck and shoulders, and you feel stiff and perhaps achy. Some of the effects of that tension can manifest in the body as tension headaches, eye strain, back pain and exhaustion. Exercise will help reduce that stiffness and give more ease and comfort in your body.

4   Regular exercise has a positive effect on the mood and emotions

because our body releases endorphins, the 'feelgood' chemicals that make us feel more positive and energized. They are the body's own natural antidepressants and can help us feel calmer because most people, when exercising, do not worry. You are focused on the physical activity and so the nerve cells in the brain that cause us to worry are actually more at rest when we exercise. The effect of this is to allow those cells time to renew their stores of the positive chemical messengers, so they can function normally the next time they are needed.

One final benefit of exercise is that we can decide what effect we want it to have, and choose the exercise method to produce that for us. What you choose will obviously depend on your personal preferences, but it should be pleasurable and not something you are going to be willing to put off because you don't enjoy it. Find an exercise that you find some enjoyment in, and if you can also have the company of others to support you, then so much the better. Ideally if you can manage it, look at starting to exercise for around three times a week for 20 minutes and gradually increase that if it is comfortable and possible for you to fit into your week. No matter how little you can manage, there will be definite health benefits, including getting a better night's sleep. To most effectively include exercise regularly into your life, try some of these suggestions:

- Decide what end result you want. Because exercise can both have a tranquillizing or an energizing effect, think of the difference between yoga and aerobics, then select according to your needs. If you are restless and agitated, then a high-powered gym workout might burn off some off that excess adrenaline, but you also might feel that a more tranquil regime would suit you. You decide, and try both at different times to see what works best. If your stress response is to be listless and apathetic, then you may want to try something more energetic to raise your mood like aerobics, or something gentler like yoga.
- Keep it simple. If your preferred exercise routine depends on driving 30 minutes to the local gym or pool, be realistic about how often you are likely to do that, especially if you are tired and already have too full a schedule to fulfil. Try to find something that will not add to your workload, because if you then don't manage to

exercise you are likely to feel guilty, and that is just more stress.

- Experiment and find out what is the best time of day for you to exercise. Are you slow to get going in the morning, or a lark that would be happy out for a dawn walk? Are you able to spend part of your lunch break at a local gym or swimming pool, or do some tai chi in the park?

- Look for hidden opportunities to exercise. Get off the bus a stop earlier, walk up the stairs instead of using the lift, stand instead of sit when you make some of your telephone calls and if you can, move around so you are taking some very gentle, but consistent exercise.

- Be realistic about the time you have available to exercise. Is there time in the week, or do you really only have free time at the weekends? If your time is really committed, can you find just ten minutes a day to do some simple stretching or breathing exercises? BUT. . .

- Be honest with yourself about what time you really have available. If you spend three hours every evening watching television you could probably find time to exercise in that period as well. A week has 168 hours in it, and you really only need to exercise for three 20-minute sessions a week. One hour out of 168 shouldn't be too hard to find if you are serious about reducing your stress levels.

Once you have decided on how to incorporate exercise into your life, you might want to consider what exactly you want to do. You might want to go back to a sport or pastime you enjoyed in the past like dancing, cricket or tennis, or try something new like golf, yoga, aerobics or jogging.

The golden rule is to start slowly and gradually increase the amount, or pace, of the exercise you are doing. If you haven't played football in ten years, then don't sign up for a Sunday side that plays for two hours at a hard pace, but perhaps start doing the stamina and flexibility exercises that will help you build up to that. Most local authorities have a huge variety of fitness and flexibility classes available and there are gyms and private teachers for any kind of exercise you might want. Do a little bit of research to find out what is available in your area, and what you can manage within your current physical condition and available time.

Exercise systems fall roughly into two categories: those that are more aerobic and high energy in nature, and those that are gentler and more relaxing. There are some that combine elements of both and here are some suggestions if you need some help deciding where to start.

Exercise to Calm the Mind and Body

Walking

Perhaps surprisingly one of the most easily available exercises is one that you do every day, without even thinking about it, and that is just walking. You don't need any special equipment, just put on some training or supportive shoes and head out of the door. Walking at a steady, regular pace is recommended for anyone who needs to relax. The dual action of the freeing of the mind and the improvement in your circulation can help raise both your energy levels and your mood. The pace you walk at is entirely up to you; if you feel as though you need to burn off some of that adrenaline then you can power walk, punching your arms back and forth and picking up a good pace. If you are new to any form of exercise then a gentle stroll is fine too; just keep walking and breathe naturally and easily and you will start to feel more relaxed. If you don't have anywhere near your home that you want to walk in then head for the local park, or follow the example of American senior citizens who head for their nearest shopping mall where they can walk round in comfort and safety without having to worry about the vagaries of the weather. Just take every opportunity to walk every day because a Californian study suggests that a regular, brisk walk can have as great an effect on calming the nerves as taking a 400 mg dose of a tranquillizer.

Yoga

Yoga is perhaps the most well-known exercise system for reducing stress. It has been practised for thousands of years for fitness of body, calmness of mind and improved circulation. There are many different types of yoga, from the dynamic to the meditative, so check out which is most suitable for you.

Hatha yoga is perhaps the best known and most widely available and is suitable for most people, particularly for those wanting more flexibility and to improve their muscle strength.

Iyengar and the newer Ashtanga yoga are more dynamic and aerobic and demand a higher initial standard of fitness than Hatha yoga. Whatever form you choose will involve learning about using the breath to control stress and reduce anxiety and tension. Although there are many videos and books available on yoga, it is better initially to take a class with a qualified teacher.

Tai Chi and Qi Gong

Tai chi and qi gong also come from the tradition of Eastern philsosophy and well-being, but this time from China rather than India. Originally developed as a martial art, the modern-day practice focuses on the very positive mental and physical benefits from these slow, almost ballet-like movements and they are practised in China by people well into their eighties and nineties who maintain their health and flexibility in this way.

Practice of qi gong often precedes a tai chi class and consists of a very relaxing series of gentle flowing and repetitive movements of the arms. At the same time, breathing is slowed down to a deeper, more gentle rhythm, and this helps to focus the mind and maintain concentration.

Tai chi itself is similar, but involves a greater range of graceful dance-like movements. There are many different styles, and the number of postures vary so that the practice of the whole form can take as little as ten minutes or as long as an hour, so again speak to the teacher about whether this is suitable for you. Tai chi rebalances energy levels and brings greater peace and harmony to mind and body. Regular tai chi practice is said to result in increased joint mobility, better posture, improved circulation and more flexible muscles. Both tai chi and qi gong can be practised at any age and level of fitness, but it is important to learn them through a recognized practitioner.

Exercise to Energize the Body and Mind

The key here is to find an exercise that raises your energy levels, but doesn't overtax your body. If you are unable to hold a conversation while exercising then you are probably pushing too hard. The 'high' that many people experience after exercising is very attractive, and it is that release of feel-good endorphins that you are after, but a workaholic attitude to exercise is counterproductive and only produces more stress for the body. So whatever exercise you choose, remember that the object is to enjoy it and feel good afterwards; overdoing it will put more strain on your body and undercut the good stress reduction benefits that regular exercise can bring.

Attitude is very important when it comes to exercising. Some types can be both energizing and calm-inducing and a lot can depend on how you approach them. Golf involves plenty of walking and general exercise, which is definitely calming, but if you are very competitive about your game or worried about your performance then it is likely to be more stressful than relaxing. Swimming, too, is a wonderful cardio vascular workout, and the repetitive nature of doing laps is very relaxing for some people if taken at a regular, calm pace. However, if you push yourself to swim more than is comfortable for your body, or at a faster pace, or set yourself targets for laps that you can't meet, then again you are likely to add to your stress rather than reduce it.

There is a wide range of exercise routines that are higher in energy output, so try out a few to see what suits you. Going regularly to a gym works wonders for some people, but first check that it is staffed by qualified instructors and make sure you have a thorough fitness assessment before any routine is devised for you. This should be tailored to your specific needs, and altered and adapted as your fitness level increases.

If the gym isn't for you, there is a range of sports like football, tennis, badminton, squash or golf. Or you might prefer to take an aerobics class or find a local pool and take your exercise in the water. Exercising with others makes it more enjoyable, and doesn't have to be called 'exercise' to give you a good workout. If you like to dance, then join a class and revive your ballroom skills or learn a new dance like salsa. If you haven't got a partner, try one of the forms of dancing that doesn't need one, like line dancing, or circle or folk dancing. If finding a regular time to exercise is a problem, and it's hard to commit to a class or club, then there are also plenty of exercise and dance workout videos to suit all levels of fitness and expertise, and you can make the most of your time at home.

If your problem with exercising is that you get bored, then try a 'mix and match' approach of several types to keep you stimulated.

Walk one day, go to a dance class one week and swimming the next, whatever you will enjoy, and maintain, is the right exercise for you. If you are not certain about what kind of exercise is right for you, talk to your doctor to see what they recommend for the kind of stress symptoms that you have.

Chapter Nine

Lifestyle Changes

Stress can often cause the breakdown of our normal routines. We don't eat properly, we aren't sleeping well and there is just too much to do in any one day. Establishing a regular routine will help you feel more in control and therefore less stressed. Try to establish a good diet with not too many stimulants or overuse of tobacco or alcohol. If you are not sleeping well, don't stay up late at night until you hope you will be tired; instead try to maintain a regular time that you go to bed and get up each day and this will help your internal body clock

Look at what you have to fit into a day and realistically try to establish priorities. What is essential, what would be good to do and what could be postponed? Prioritize so that you tackle the important things first and get a sense of achievement from finishing something rather than trying to do too many things at once.

Does your stress come from too many people making demands on you so that you often find yourself saying 'yes' when in fact you mean 'no'? Are you always late for things? Do you get frustrated knowing you could have done a better job if you had organized your time better? If these apply to you, then it might be helpful to look at what changes you could make to simplify your daily routine. If saying no is a problem, then that is something that won't change overnight, and you might want to get some expert help from an assertiveness management course or book. The tip here is to start saying no to small and relatively unimportant things that have no real emotional impact for you. This way you get to practise in safety, and it is much easier saying no to things like an extra cup of coffee or not taking a free leaflet from someone in the street. A polite but clear 'no thank you' might take a bit of practice, but definitely gets easier the more you do it.

If the problem is saying no to someone else's demands, and you don't want to do what they request or can't manage anything extra, then try saying 'Thank you for asking me but it just isn't possible at the moment'. Stress often comes when we try to justify our actions, and a simple change we can make is to stop doing that as much as possible. It may be a hard habit to break, but you don't have to give reasons for your refusal to do anything; it's your right just to say no without having to justify it. It might take a bit of practice, but it is definitely a stress reducer.

Have you got into a routine where you 'always' do certain tasks or chores and they are now proving heavy going? Again look realistically at what you could change. Do you always cook dinner when you get home from work? Could someone else in the family do it one night a week, or what about having a takeaway instead? Are you the one who uses up their lunch hour to go to the post office, replenish the office tea and biscuit supply or is responsible for cards and collections for staff events like leaving parties or get well flowers? Well, again, couldn't someone else take over for a while? Think about who you could ask, and if no one is willing to take it on, then why don't you just stop doing it for a while and see what happens? Saying clearly that you need a break because you have got too much else on is a positive step forward, and is also a good way to practise saying no and not justifying.

Is one of the problems that actually you are overstretched and working too many hours? In England we have some of the longest working weeks in Europe, and if you are putting in more than the average 40-hour week then you are placing additional strain on your body and its ability to recover.

Time management is not just a tool for executives, it is simply a good way of organizing time to serve you best. You need to have a diary that allows you space to write in your daily activities for a week, and then sit down and look at where the biggest chunks of your time go and how you spend the day. At the beginning of the week make a master list of the things that must be done that week and use it as a checklist each day to focus on what to tackle first. Remember that it is not always possible to get everything done and you are human, so allow yourself some leeway. If you like, you can categorize the tasks as A, B, C in order of importance and then you have a clear indication of what you need to do first. The 'A' list is usually the urgent and essential tasks, the 'B' list is important but not as urgent and the 'C' list is neither urgent nor of high priority but will need to be done at some stage. An example of an 'A' task would be ringing the plumber if you have a burst pipe, a 'B' task would be contacting the insurance company about the damage and a 'C' task would be finding a decorator to repair the damage.

Time management is not just about prioritizing work, it refers to the rest of your life as well. If you are someone who regularly works through the lunch hour, then that would be another good place to start. Mind and body need a break away from the desk and a brisk walk outside, or even up and down the stairs, will give you a quick energy boost. If you have a walkman, put in a tape or CD of your favourite relaxing music and use that while you walk or sit in the park to give you some mental peace and distance from your work problems. Also look at your diary and see if the things that you enjoy, like socializing or sport, always get pushed out to make room for more work. To be healthy you need to have a balanced life that incorporates work, rest and play, so it comes back to prioritizing. Try to find where you can take some time off, and if you really want to go dancing once a week or out to the cinema, don't leave it to chance. If you write it into your diary as a genuine appointment you are less likely to cancel it.

Are you stressed because your mind is always active and worrying away at something or another? Well, the mind is like the lungs and heart, it never stops being on duty but it can be lulled into quietness by certain activities. If you need to rest your mind, then doing something that occupies you fully on one activity, like reading or meditating, will help because you have something else to focus on. Many people find working with their hands has this effect too, from the simple repetitive tasks like ironing, gardening or cooking to engaging with a hobby or craft or playing a musical instrument. All of these will help to reduce the mind's chatter because any activity which concentrates your attention on something other than your worries is giving the 'problem-solving' area of the brain a chance to rest. Because it isn't having to keep that active, then the brain gets a chance to divert its activity into producing more of the positive chemical messengers that you need to reduce your stress levels.

Chapter Ten

Stress Management

People who effectively manage stress consider life a challenge that can be enjoyed, rather than a series of irritations that they can't quite cope with. If you are feeling in control of your life, no matter what the problems and setbacks may be, then you are not likely to be seriously affected by stress. When looking at the questionnaire earlier in the book, did you notice what really caused you stress recently? Was it mainly external events like divorce or redundancy or did it come from you having unrealistic expectations of yourself and others? Self-knowledge is vital to really tackling stress effectively.

Identify the Problem

There are many stress management techniques that can be used, and first it will help to identify what the main problem area is. A good exercise to find out is to ask yourself the five 'W' questions:

1   What is the main problem?
2   Who is the problem?
3   Where does it mainly occur?
4   Why does it happen?
5   When does it generally happen?

Write down your thoughts on a piece of paper, and although you may not get all the answers straight away, keep going back to it and adding or clarifying what you have written. If you are still not sure, then if you have kept up your food and mood diary, go back to that and see when your stress symptoms cropped up and if they were tied to any specific event. For instance, if you get a migraine after presenting the monthly accounts to your manager, then that is a fairly clear area to start exploring, but if it is more vague then you need to spend a bit more time in quiet reflection and this exercise might help you to identify the real problem that you haven't been able to see clearly before.

The aim of stress management is to help you get that balance between work, rest and play that we all need. This involves all aspects of our lives including the physical, intellectual and emotional aspects of life. These strategies can help you start managing how you deal with stress.

Control Your Mind

Stress and pressure makes us more likely to misinterpret events, and usually in a negative fashion. We see a distorted picture of what is going on and, over time, we come to accept that as the truth. What we think affects how we feel, and that affects our mood, but we can learn to think differently and more positively about our situation.

It is important to remember that our moods are created by what we think about what has happened to us, and not about the actual event itself. For instance, if you get to the cinema too late to see the film you had chosen, you can either decide that your evening is ruined and get cross and irritable about it, or think that it's a great opportunity to try a new film you might not have considered that starts a bit later, or do something completely different instead. The event is the same – missing the start of the film – but your reaction to it can be different. And you can choose to change your mind. If you normally would be upset, make a positive decision to be glad about it and see what difference that makes to your mood. It's your choice whether you see it positively or negatively, and usually you make these kinds of 'feeling' decisions based on your previous experience.

In a stressed or depressed state of mind we unfortunately have a tendency to pay more attention to our negative thoughts and it is entirely possible to think yourself into feeling more sad and unhappy than you possibly are. The saying that 'misery loves company' is not entirely without foundation because when we are feeling bad, we go back into our memory and remember all the other times we felt like this. This downward spiral is very common and, to break out of it, you need to pay attention to how you respond so that you can change your future behaviour. You can do this by thinking very consciously of a good, positive and happy memory and decide to focus on that instead. Try it and you will see a difference in your mood.

Make it Manageable

If you feel that there is just too much to do, write out each task and then break it down into smaller and more manageable pieces. For instance, the task might be filling in a tax return which you find daunting and so you keep putting it off. Every time you think about it doing it you remember how overwhelming it feels and put it off yet again. This is highly stressful, and one way round it is to break it down. Try writing out under the heading of 'filling in the tax return' all the things you need to do to complete it. For instance, first you need to find the form, then assemble the various paperwork you need, again make it separate tasks like get the bank statements, the building society statements, the mortgage details, the receipts or invoices that you might have to submit. And do just one task at a time so it is manageable. Start with finding the form, then add the various pieces of paper to the same file. The final event is filling it in. You can allocate only a short period of time to each task, say 10 to 15 minutes, so that it seems possible rather than too much. This technique can be applied to any task. It is just looking at what you need to do and tackling only one part of it at a time. This way you get a sense of achievement about each thing done, not a sense of failure about not tackling it. That in itself will reduce the stress around it.

Learn to Delegate

You are not solely responsible for everything that happens. Let someone else take over some of the jobs, especially the ones you don't like. If you hate washing the car, but spend every Sunday morning doing it, then pay another family member to do it and spend that time going for a walk or working on a hobby that will relax you. There are many tasks at home and at work that can be shared; even if you wash the car yourself only every other Sunday, that would be an improvement, wouldn't it? Particularly watch out for doing regular tasks just because you have always done them; having a routine meeting with your staff every Monday morning may be vital, or it could just be a habit that you have fallen into, and holding the meeting fortnightly or monthly to keep staff updated might work just as well.

Progress Not Perfection

When you have so many tasks that you are starting to feel overwhelmed, it could be time to look at how you approach them. Are you someone who always has to have it absolutely right, or can you accept that sometimes in order to get the job done it might have to be less than perfect? If you are a perfectionist, that in itself can be stressful because you will never be completely satisfied with what you have achieved. It may also mean that you don't want to show others your vulnerability or ask for help if you are stuck, so you deprive yourself of some valuable support which could make a lot of difference to how well you cope with a stressful situation.

If your watchword is 'progress not perfection' then the emphasis is on moving forward, at a pace that is comfortable and that adequately gets the job done. It may not be perfect, but then very little in life is, and by relaxing your standards you will also be reducing your stress.

Controlling perfectionist behaviour may take some time, but it can be done. There are four ways in which you could start to tackle it. First, make a list of how your perfectionist attitudes are helpful to you, and where they hold you back, so you can see exactly how they are affecting your life. Next, set some boundaries around the tasks that you are undertaking so you curb the potential for keeping at it until you feel it is perfect. For instance, if you have to write a letter, set a clear deadline for it and stick to it. Be realistic; your perfect letter might take an hour to write, but an adequate one could probably be done in at least half that time, if not less. Don't be afraid to admit that you are unsure about your abilities in any situation, or that you are nervous or worried about it. You are not superman or superwoman, and we all have situations where we feel unable to match up to our own, or others', expectations.

Sharing your worries with a close family member or friend will help you recognize that you are just as human and vulnerable as the rest of us. Rather than focusing on the perfect end result that you want, enjoy what you are doing in each moment and see each action as a positive move forward towards that end result.

Slowing Down The Pace

If you are someone who is highly competitive, frustrated if you are delayed in any way, edgy and impatient, then you are what is classed as an 'A' type personality and the most important stress management tool for you is to learn to slow down. This kind of behaviour means that you are constantly stimulating the body to produce large amounts of adrenaline. The health problems associated with high levels of adrenaline are stress, heart disease, stomach ulcers and strokes, so it essential to take action to change this habitual pattern.

Self-awareness is the starting point; notice whether you race through meetings, dash up the stairs, bolt down your food as quickly as possible, or anything similarly fast paced. Any of these activities can be slowed down; you can choose to deliberately walk, eat and even speak more slowly to give a greater sense of calm. Go through your diary to see if you can take out even one of your scheduled activities to give you some breathing space and try never to schedule meetings or events so close together that realistically you have not got time to get between them without rushing.

Relaxation is not an optional extra; you can build it into your life if you make an effort to do so. If you always work through lunch and coffee breaks, make the effort to leave at least one or two a week free so you can use that time to go for a walk, or close your door and do five minutes of stretches, deep breaths or just yawn to slow your body down.

Type 'A' people are often multi-taskers; they like the challenge of doing several things at once and being seen to be able to do so. Break the pattern by focusing on just one thing at a time and try saying no to some of the requests you get – you don't have to do it all.

Make a note when you get angry or frustrated and see if there are common situations that trigger you. Is it always in a traffic jam or when someone turns up late for an appointment? When you know what the trigger is you can start to take action to avoid that person or situation and find ways of dealing with it that are less stressful than your current behaviour.

Practise Relaxation

We will look at relaxation methods in more detail in the next chapter, but initially just taking some deep breaths to calm you down will instantly reduce your stress levels. Start the day by stretching out in bed before you get up, and continue to stretch throughout the day at regular intervals. Stand up frequently and stretch your arms over your head throughout the day, gently roll your neck from side to side and swing your arms across your body and back again. All these will help to release the tension that accumulates in the muscles. Try to find ways to include some form of relaxation into your daily life, even if it is just a minute to look out of the window and see the sky.

Keep Things in Perspective

Trying to keep things in perspective can be very hard to do when you are stressed, but try to maintain your sense of humour and find something to celebrate, laugh at and enjoy every day. If you have a difficult colleague or family member, remember that it is not just you who is affected by their behaviour, and you have a choice about how much you let it get to you. No matter what is going on there is time to enjoy a beautiful view, appreciate a good meal or a conversation with a friend and try to offset these good events against the things that stress you.

Get Outside Support

Sharing what is going with your family, a close friend, minister, counsellor or your doctor is a very good way of defusing the tension, giving yourself space and letting someone else share the burden. We can feel very isolated and not want to bother other people, though actually they usually have a pretty good idea of what is going on. Sharing your thoughts and fears can help you get a more realistic view the situation and perhaps show you some options that you hadn't considered for yourself.

Take it One Day at a Time

Rome wasn't built in a day and reducing or eliminating stress that may have been accumulating for years can take some time. Long-term change is best achieved slowly, one step at a time. You don't want the added stress of thinking you are not doing enough to change your situation, so be patient and you will see real changes. Be kind to yourself and start each day with the intention of doing the best you can, and being realistic about what you can achieve. Think about whatever you would most like to change, and then try to take one small action every day that will move you towards that. For instance, if you have a specific goal like 'reducing my blood pressure' then think of all the things you can do that will help that. You might decide to walk for an extra five minutes every day, or reduce the amount of salt you put on your food. It doesn't have to be a huge action; you just need to take it consistently, one day at a time.

Chapter Eleven

Time to Relax

It is surprising how guilty we can feel about 'doing nothing' and yet it is essential for your health and well-being to have a period of relaxation every day. When we are stressed and overwhelmed by life we feel even less like taking time off for relaxing because we feel can't cope with all we have to do, and surely it would be worse if we start adding in relaxation time? Well, no it wouldn't, because we all need to turn off from time to time and unless you do so your stress levels will increase, not decrease.

The fear of being selfish and taking time for ourselves is quite deeply ingrained in our culture, but there is a lot to be said for this kind of personal selfishness. We worry about letting other people down, but we let ourselves down all the time. It is not selfish to allow your body time to renew and repair itself or to give your mind 'time off' from constant worry and anxiety.

Find something that you enjoy and that can be fitted into your life easily on a regular basis. For some people that might be sitting in an armchair and reading a book or listening to music, or running a bath and putting in some relaxing essential oils such as lavender and rose. If your mind is always busy, then doing a crossword or a jigsaw puzzle is relaxing if it focuses your mind on something other than your immediate worries and concerns, but not if you set yourself to do it in a tight timeframe and make it into a competition! You could learn to do yoga or to meditate, or find a hobby that absorbs you; whatever you choose make sure it is really relaxing, though your definition of it might vary from someone else's.

Make a Place to Relax

Another important way of relaxing is to make sure that you have somewhere in your home that is tranquil and restful so that it can be a real sanctuary when you are under stress. If your living space is cluttered and messy, then visually that will crowd in on you and make you feel more pressured, so try to keep it clear and welcoming. Make sure you have some restful music or candles to create a good atmosphere, and let others know when you need to have some quiet time by yourself. If your house is always busy and full of people coming and going then it is even more essential that you make a quiet place for yourself. It could be your bedroom, and if that's your choice for a place to relax then make sure it is warm, comfortable and nurturing. Banish the television or any electronic equipment like a computer that might distract you, and burn a relaxing lavender candle or essential oil to help you start to unwind. Lowering the lights will automatically help your body to start to relax, so turn off the overhead lights and just have a side lamp or candles. If your bedroom isn't suitable, then what about the bathroom? A long warm bath can be very soothing; just lock the door, use your favourite bath oil and lie back and relax. Bathroom lighting tends to be quite harsh, so try lighting some candles instead and perhaps have a relaxation tape or music playing. You could also try some of these techniques to find something that can help you to relax even more.

Follow Your Breath

The Eastern traditions believe that the breath is a bridge between the conscious mind and the functioning of the body. We normally don't control our breath; it is totally automatic and generally happens without our even noticing, unless we are stressed or exerting ourselves. But we can control our breath and by so doing we can also change the state of our body from a normal to a resting state. We can change it just by paying attention to it, without doing anything else, and what could be simpler than that? Sit comfortably in a chair, or lie on a bed or couch, and close your eyes. You are going to do absolutely nothing other than just breathe in and out and put your focus on that breath. Don't attempt to control it, just follow your breath with your mind and you will start to feel your body relaxing. If your mind starts to wander, just gently refocus and if you find it difficult to stop thoughts popping into your head, try saying to yourself 'breathing in' when you breathe in and 'breathing out' when you breathe out. Keep this going for a few minutes and if you start to feel any tension in your body think about your breath moving to that area and allowing it to release the tension. You might find yourself taking deep sighs as the slow rhythm of your breathing relaxes your whole body. This exercise will help you feel calm, even when done for just a short period like a minute or so. If you have trouble relaxing at night, try this exercise in bed and it will help calm you ready for sleep.

Muscle Relaxant

Pick somewhere warm where you won't be disturbed and put a blanket or rug on the floor. Lie on your back with your hands facing palm up towards the ceiling. You are going to tense and relax all the muscles of your body in turn and it will take around 20 minutes to complete. You can put on some calming music if you like, and begin by just taking four or five normal breaths as you get comfortable. You will tense each muscle and hold that for a slow count of five, then release it and rest for a slow count of ten, and then repeat the sequence again with that muscle. Use this sequence:

- *Hands*: clench and unclench your fists.
- *Arms*: pull them in towards your body, but relax your hands.
- *Shoulders*: pull them both up towards your ears and drop them down again.
- *Forehead*: raise your eyebrows and wrinkle your forehead.
- *Eyes*: screw your eyes tightly shut and then open them wide.
- *Jaw*: press your back teeth hard together.
- *Lips*: press your lips and front teeth together.
- *Face*: screw up your entire face as hard as you can.
- *Neck*: first stretch up your chin so your neck is pushed back, then pull your chin forwards onto your chest.
- *Stomach*: pull in your stomach muscles towards your spine.
- *Buttocks*: clench tightly together.
- *Thighs*: push your heels hard into the floor.
- *Calves*: extend your feet and point your toes.
- *Feet*: draw up your toes and clench them.

As you get more familiar with this exercise, you can also imagine the tension being released from the muscles as you relax them and let them go.

Peripheral Vision

This exercise seems to activate the parasympathetic nervous system; the part of your nervous system that calms and slows you down. It helps your mind, body and emotions to come back into balance. If you have ever studied tai chi, they talk about 'soft focus' of the eyes as a way of letting go of tension and withdrawing attention back into the body in order to relax it. It's the difference between fixedly staring hard at something, and almost letting your eyes semi-close so that things look softer and a little out of focus.

Sitting comfortably in a chair, look ahead of you and find a spot on the wall that is just a little above your eye level. If you don't have a point to focus on, if it's a plain wall, then try putting a Post-it note on the wall with a cross or circle marked on it. You are going to be looking at this throughout, allowing your eyes to soften so the image may seem a little blurred. You will notice that the room seems to recede and it is almost as if you are looking down a tunnel. Still focusing on the same point, allow your field of vision to get bigger and start to notice more and more of what is to either side of that point. Now you are also paying attention to what you can see out of the corners of your eyes on each side, then expand your senses to see if you can feel or be aware of anything behind you as well. While you are doing this exercise, you may notice that your breathing has moved lower down in your chest and perhaps slowed down or become deeper, and the face and jaw muscles will also start to relax. When you are ready, just let your field of vision gradually refocus and return to normal

If you practise this, you will soon have no need to use the point on the wall but will be able to change your peripheral vision wherever you are. If you have 'stage fright' or are nervous about speaking in meetings or have to give a speech, then learning to go into peripheral vision can be very useful for calming any pre-audience nerves. Or if your mind is ceaselessly giving you negative messages, this again can block out that voice and let you gain some inner peace and tranquillity.

Body Attention

Martial arts and yoga practitioners know that where you focus your attention in the body has a big effect on how you feel. It is known as 'centring' and to do it you start by standing up in a relaxed fashion, with your feet parallel and about shoulder width apart. Place one of your hands over your stomach so that the index finger is directly over your navel; now look down to where your ring finger is resting and imagine a point at that level right in the middle of your body. In the martial arts traditions this is the centre of power in your body and is known as the 'tan-tien' in the Chinese tradition.

As in the previous exercise, let your eyes soften and go into peripheral vision, allow your body to relax, and make sure your knees aren't locked. Keep your attention focused on that central point inside your body and continue to breathe easily and regularly, again noticing where you are holding tension.

This level of focus blocks out worry, panic and fear and is very useful to practise if you suffer from anxiety or panic attacks. You can use it anywhere because the point is in the focus inside the body. You don't have to be standing still or sitting; just allow your attention to go 100 per cent to that spot.

A Protective Shield

If things seem to be just too much for you to cope with and one more thing is unbearable, then this technique can be helpful to distance you from the confusion and chaos that goes on in the outside world. It might seem a little strange, but it does work. Imagine that you are sitting in the centre of a clear bubble which is acting as a protective shield between you and the outside world. This bubble is transparent so you can see what is going on, but it is also very, very strong so that everything stressful that happens outside just bounces off and away from you, leaving you calm and still inside the bubble. So the more stressful it is outside, the calmer you are inside.

This exercise works because your unconscious mind doesn't distinguish between imagination and 'reality', so that if you imagine that you are shielded from stress, you will feel exactly as if you are being shielded and protected from it. Again, it can be a helpful exercise if you are nervous about public speaking; just extend the bubble to cover the whole room and let yourself know that nothing outside can get in to disturb your concentration or upset your presentation.

Become Detached

Sometimes in emotionally fraught situations, or if there is an argument or disagreement that is upsetting you, it can be helpful to use this very simple technique to detach or distance yourself from what is going on. It helps you get a clearer perspective and stay calm by literally allowing yourself to float above the situation.

Imagine that you are floating up and out of your body, higher and higher, as far up as you feel comfortable and where you are able to look down on yourself. What you will notice is that the higher up you float, the more detached and calm you will feel.

These are some techniques that you can try at home, and there are also many classes available in meditation and relaxation if you would like to explore some more options.

Chapter Twelve

AlternativeTherapies and Remedies

In addition to the many self-help methods available to deal with stress, sometimes extra help that is needed and alternative therapies and remedies are frequently used to assist stress reduction. Some of these may be familiar to you, others may be new, but the ones listed here are either helpful for general stress reduction or to relieve specific symptoms or behaviours around stress.

Alternative, or complementary, treatments include a vast range of therapies, some of which have been around for thousands of years, like herbal medicine and acupuncture, and more recent newcomers like homoeopathy and hypnotherapy. What they all have in common is that they treat the patient as a whole person rather than treating just one specific symptom or range of symptoms. This means that your initial consultation with such a practitioner can last for up to an hour as they will want to know what is going on for you on the physical, mental and emotional levels, and in all areas of your life, so as best to be able to help you.

Acupuncture

Originating in China, acupuncture is used worldwide for stress reduction and pain relief. Practitioners have to undergo a rigorous training programme – some of up to seven years. Fine needles are inserted into the body at what have been identified as the meridians, or energy centres, and their aim is to unblock or harmonize the energy that is continually circulating in the body. This treatment is believed to stimulate the brain's production of its own natural painkillers and positive mood enhancers, so reducing stress.

Aromatherapy

Using essential oils can either relax, stimulate or re-energize the mind by being absorbed through the skin or directly inhaled. They are not just a nice smell, but have definite healing qualities which help emotional well-being. Pure plant oils are very potent and need to be diluted in some way, so are most often used in a bath, a massage oil or a vaporizer to dispel the fragrance into the room. They are never for internal use. A qualified aromatherapist will help you decide which single, or combination, of oils would be best for you, and they are also freely available to buy over the counter. Before using any oil, do read the label to make sure it has the qualities that you require, and note that some oils carry health warnings. For instance, you should not use parsley or camphor oils if you are pregnant as they can trigger a miscarriage, and if you love to sunbathe then avoid bergamot and lemon oils as they make your skin more sensitive to the sun and you will burn more easily. Frequently used oils are: lavender for calming, balancing, and helping with insomnia; frankincense for improving mood and concentration; and jasmine for a tonic effect and to help with depression.

Ayurveda

Ayurveda is an ancient Indian system of preventative medicine and starts from an analysis of four basic body types on which treatment is based. This is a very comprehensive form of medicine, which, as well as recommending specific herbal remedies, can also include suggestions for diet, breathing and exercise, including yoga and meditation.

Bach Flowers

These remedies were developed by Dr Bach, a Harley Street consultant, as an offshoot of homoeopathic medicine. They consist of concentrated plant and flower essences which are made into an original tincture, which is then diluted and stored in water and alcohol in small glass bottles. They are taken by putting several drops direct on the tongue or in a glass of water. They do not treat physical conditions, but the underlying emotional causes of them and so are beneficial when treating stress. There are 38 separate remedies for specific conditions: rock rose and mimulus for apprehension and anxiety, holly and beech for impatience and intolerance, for example. There are practitioners who will advise on the single or combination of remedies that will be most effective, but for general use the Rescue Remedy combination is widely available. As its name suggests, it can be an effective treatment for mood swings and emotional conditions.

Chiropractic and Osteopathy

Stress causes our muscles to tense and this tension can affect our posture, leading to pain in the back, shoulders and neck. Because the spine is the conduit from the brain for our nervous system, any misalignment can pinch the nerves or reduce the blood supply and cause pain, stiffness and discomfort. Manipulation of the spine can release this tension and realign our body to be in better balance. There are different types of osteopathy and chiropractic including McTimoney chiropractic, which is a more subtle adjustment of the body, and cranial osteopathy where the head is gently held and adjusted to release tension in the head and neck. All of them are beneficial to release stiffness and reduce pain caused by tension and stress.

Counselling

Counselling is now so popular that it is widely available on the NHS and many medical practices have a counsellor working in them. Simply talking about your problems and what is causing you stress is sometimes enough to make the difference between coping with it and feeling overwhelmed. Interestingly, younger people are better at talking things through than their elders. One in three young people suffering from stress will call a friend to talk about it, but these figures fall to less than one in ten as we get older. There is no doubt that sharing a worry does help get it into perspective and it can be very helpful to be able to identify the cause of your stress. You may find that the counsellor offers you a new perspective on the problem that will enable you to look at it differently, and perhaps also respond to it differently. Counsellors in doctors' surgeries will be qualified and registered; if you want to find a counsellor privately, make sure they also have the same qualifications.

Herbal Medicine

Herbal medicine is found in every culture in the world and is one of the oldest healing systems known. There are English, Chinese and Indian herbal practitioners, and each system has their own different training and professional registration. Herbs are natural, but not harmless; in fact they contain some very powerfully acting substances, so you must seek advice from an appropriately qualified practitioner. Do not attempt to self-treat with fresh herbs as it is easy to mistake one common herb for another, and a mistake can be dangerous, or even fatal. There are many proprietary herbal medicines available through health shops and pharmacies that are specifically designed to treat stress and are both safe and effective. They may contain some of the sedative and calming herbs such as valerian, hops, lemon balm, passiflora, gentian, wild lettuce and motherwort.

Flotation

A relatively new therapy, flotation, involves lying in a few inches of warm water that has been saturated with Epsom salts and so is extremely buoyant. Flotation is normally done in a darkened pool or tank, usually specially designed for the purpose. It is believed to achieve a better balance between the left and right cortex of the brain and many people find it be deeply relaxing emotionally, as well allowing the body to relax as it is fully supported in the water.

Homoeopathy

One of the most widely used therapies, homoeopathy is also one of the few complementary medicine systems that can be available on the NHS. It has been accepted and established for many years, and the Royal Family are known to regularly use homoeopathic remedies. Generally the remedies come in the form of very small tablets, which are put under the tongue to dissolve, and they work by treating symptoms with a remedy that stimulates the body to repair itself. Because it relies very much on the whole picture of the person, including your physical build and colouring, the remedy for stress may be quite different from one person to another and you are recommended to consult with a practitioner for an individual prescription. A number of doctors are also qualified homoeopaths, and your GP can refer you to a homoeopathic hospital for treatment. They may also have a list of local practitioners who work with the surgery if they are not qualified in that way themselves. There are many over-the-counter homoeopathic remedies available and these may be helpful specifically for stress: aconite for anxiety and restlessness; kalium phosphoricum to support the body to deal with mental and physical exhaustion; and nux vomica for nervous indigestion, nausea and stomach upsets. Because the active ingredient in homoeopathic remedies is so small, they are perfectly safe to take and there is no known evidence of either side effects or overdose.

Hypnotherapy

Perhaps best known for helping people lose weight or give up smoking, hypnotherapy can be highly effective in treating both the causes and symptoms of stress. It is a very relaxing therapy, which puts you into a light meditative state where your breathing slows down and, although in a light trance, you are not unconscious and therefore are aware of what is going on around you. It is recommended for stress reduction generally, and also for the fear, anxiety, panic conditions and palpitations that can be some of the most distressing symptoms. Always look for a qualified hypnotherapist; again, your doctor may refer you to a medical or clinical hypnotherapist as they undergo a strict training and often work in conjunction with doctors or a medical practice.

Kinesiology

Kinesiology is a muscle-testing technique that can be used to find out which foods are most conducive to health and those which may cause unwanted allergic reactions or symptoms. If you believe you have a number of food allergies that are stressing your body it will assist you in identifying them.

Massage

A very popular treatment for a wide range of stress-related problems, massage increases the flow of blood to the muscles and skin, increases the flow of lymph which helps the body to release toxins, reduces muscular tension and assists total relaxation. A variety of massage techniques are used, including kneading, stroking and pummelling, and it can be designed to either calm or stimulate the mind and body, depending on what you require. Massage can also be combined with aromatherapy.

Meditation

Meditation is highly effective in teaching you to relax and combat stress. Practised daily for around 20 minutes, it is claimed to reduce a number of stress-related illnesses from insomnia to agitation, and one study found that regular practitioners made less than half the number of visits to a doctor than the average person who didn't meditate. It focuses on stilling the mind and controlling the breath to put the body into a deeply serene state. Meditation classes are very widely available throughout the country.

Music Therapy

Sound and music do affect our physical body, and listening to soothing music will reduce stress. There are many types of relaxation music available and you may have to experiment to find what works best for you. Two of the best known in this field include the English group Sulis, who produce music that is written to relax and de-stress the body and who took part in a clinical trial at the Bristol Cancer Clinic. This offered strong proof of significant stress reduction for both patients and families after listening to their music. The other is the international American composer and musician Jonathan Goldman, whose music is designed to soothe and relax the body, both physically and emotionally.

Nutritional Therapy

Our diet can have dramatic influences on our health and well-being, and stress can radically alter the ability of our body to process food, or to get the maximum absorption from it. A qualified nutritionist will help identify where your diet may be deficient, and can suggest specific foods, nutrients and supplements to remedy the situation. They can also use adjustments to your diet, or additional supplements, to ensure that you do not become prone to developing more stress-related symptoms, and are also able to deal more effectively with the ones you have.

Reflexology

Reflexology is the pressure and massage of points in the hands and feet to release energy blocks, on a similar principle to that of acupuncture. It works directly on all the systems of the body, especially the nervous, endocrine, circulatory and lymphatic systems and stimulates both blood flow and energy. The advantages of reflexology are that it is soothing and relaxing, and restores any imbalances held in the body. Many symptoms and health problems are stress-related and reflexology has been used for related complaints like constipation, headaches and migraines.

When looking for any practitioner, check their qualifications and whether they are nationally registered. Personal recommendation is often best, from someone who has actually used their services, but if this is not possible ask other sources such as your doctor's surgery, pharmacist, natural health clinic or store if there is anyone they know locally who has been recommended.

Chapter Thirteen

Top Tips for Handling Stress

Hopefully the information and suggestions in this book will help you begin to understand both what is causing your stress and how to start dealing with it. If you get stuck, check this list over to see if you are covering the main stress-reduction points in your life.

Stress Handling Checklist

REDUCE YOUR STRESS LOAD
Reduce the pace of change in your life.
Reduce social obligations.
Reduce work or school obligations.
Postpone changes in your living situation.
Say 'no' more often.
Eliminate possible food or environmental allergens.

TAKE POSITIVE ACTION
Make sure your diet supports you, and doesn't drain you.
Stabilize your blood sugar with complex carbohydrates and more fruit and vegetables.
Drink at least 1.5 litres of water a day.
Take any additional nutritional supplements you may need.
Exercise regularly in a way you enjoy.
Reduce stimulants like tobacco and alcohol.
Talk to your doctor about having a check-up if you feel medication could help.
See a counsellor or talk to a close friend or family member.

FIND RELAXATION TIME
Find a hobby you enjoy and make time for it.
Explore something new that will absorb you, like reading a new author, art or music.

Investigate if meditation would work for you.

Try yoga, tai chi or qi gong to combine exercise and meditation.

Listen to relaxation tapes or music and make your home a peaceful place to unwind.

Ten Tips for Reducing Your Own Personal Stress

If you want a quick boost, or to remind yourself of what you can do, then keep this list somewhere handy and start to add to it with suggestions of your own. Keep a note of the things you have found have made a real difference, and do more of them.

1   Communicate, talk and listen. Don't give up on finding someone who can help you feel better.
2   Take regular short breaks throughout the day – especially at times or in situations that are causing you to experience stress.
3   Don't force your energy up artificially with coffee and sugar, but look for more stable ways to keep your moods even.
4   Use physical activity like cleaning or washing the car to work off stress.
5   Don't put off relaxing until 'later'. It never comes.
6   When you are ill, don't pretend that you are fine, admit it and do something about it.
7   Recharge your batteries with adequate rest and sleep and don't push your body beyond its limits.
8   If faced with something that you don't like, take a deep breath and think how you could change it.
9   Recognize and acknowledge what you cannot change, and focus on those things where you can make a difference.
10 Manage your time better by learning to prioritize and delegate more.

And one final tip: learn to say NO much more often and you will keep at least some of those unnecessary pressures and stresses at bay.

Resources

For general enquiries about complementary therapies, the Institute for Complementary Medicine can provide a register of therapists:

Tel: 020 7237 5165
Website: www.icmedicine.co.uk

For information on stress management and courses, the International Stress Management Association is a registered charity:

Tel: 07000 780430
Website: http://www.isma.org.uk

Individual Therapy Associations and Contacts

Acupuncture
The British Acupuncture Council
Tel: 020 8735 0400
Website: www.acupuncture.org.uk

The British Medical Acupuncture Society
Tel: 01925 730727
Website: www.medical-acupuncture.co.uk

Aromatherapy
International Federation of Aromatherapists
Tel: 020 8742 2605
Website: www.ifparoma.org

Ayurveda
There is no single organization covering Ayurvedic practitioners in the UK, nor any national regulation of Ayurvedic herbal remedies. This link will get you information:

Website: www.interconnections.co.uk

Bach Flower Remedies
The Bach Centre
Tel: 01491 834 678
Website: www.bach-flowers.co.uk

Chiropractic and Osteopathy
British Chiropractic Association
Tel: 01189 505950
Website: www.chiropractic-uk.co.uk

Cranial Osteopathy
Details from the General Osteopathic Council
Tel: 020 7357 6655
www.osteopathy.org.uk

McTimoney Chiropractic Association
Tel: 01280 705050
Website: www.mctimoney-chiropractic.org

Counselling
British Association for Counselling
Tel: 01788 550899
Website: www.bacp.co.uk

Herbal Medicine
Register of Chinese Herbal Medicine
Tel: 01603 623994
Website: www.rchm.co.uk

Western Herbalism
National Institute of Medical Herbalists
Tel: 01392 426022
Website: www.nimh.org.uk

Flotation
Website:www.floatationTankAssociation.net

Homoeopathy
British HomoeopathicTrust
Tel: 020 7566 7800
Website: www.trusthomeopathy.org

The Society of Homoeopaths
Tel: 01604 621 400
Website: www.homeopathy-soh.org

Hypnotherapy
The British Society of Clinical Hypnosis
Tel: 020 7499 2813
Website: www.bsch.org.uk

Kinesiology
Kinesiology Federation
Tel: 08700 113545
Website: www.kinesiologyfederation.org

Massage
British MassageTherapy Council has a register of practitioners (this includes Indian Head Massage)
Tel: 01865 774123
Website: www.therapy-world.co.uk

Meditation
Transcendental Meditation Courses
Tel: 08705 143733
Website: www.t-m.org.uk

MusicTherapy
Sulis Music
Website: www.sulismusic.com

Jonathan Goldman books and music from his website
Website: www.healingsounds.com

Nutritional Therapy
British Nutrition Foundation
Tel: 020 7404 6504
Website: www.nutrition.org.uk

Institute for Optimum Nutrition
Trains nutritionists and has a national register of therapists
Tel: 0208 877 9993
Website: www.ion.ac.uk

Reflexology

The British Reflexology Association
Tel: 01886 821207
Website: www.britreflex.co.uk

Tai Chi
Classes in the UK and Ireland
Tel: 079 3938 2625
Website: www.taichifinder.co.uk

Yoga
British Wheel of Yoga
Tel: 01529 306851
Website: www.bwy.org.uk

HOW TO COPE SUCCESSFULLY WITH

ANXIETY AND DEPRESSION

Beth MacEoin

We live in stressful times and have to cope on a daily basis with a variety of different pressures. These can include financial worries, emotional stresses, bereavement, break-up of relationships and insecurity at work. When feeling well and resilient we are able to cope with a wide range of these stressful situations. It is when we become mentally and emotionally overloaded at a vulnerable time in our lives that we can suffer from symptoms of anxiety or depression. Beth MacEoin describes in her easily accessible style the various symptoms and suggests a wide range of practical measures to provide positive support.

ISBN: 1-903784-03-4   128pp

HOW TO COPE SUCCESSFULLY WITH

DEPRESSION

Dr Tom Smith

In his easily accessible style Dr Tom Smith describes depression and explains why we get depressed, the treatment with drugs together with other treatments. It shows how to think through your depression, what you can do for yourself and how to change those negative thoughts, become more outward going and assertive together with sleep problems. Depression is a serious illness that needs serious attention. Everyone in the family doctor's team has to help, the sufferer's family must also be aware of the risks and how to give assistance. Dr Tom Smith describes in this book the help you can get.

ISBN: 1903784 14 X   112pp

HOW TO COPE SUCCESSFULLY WITH

PANIC ATTACKS

Karen Sullivan

Panic attacks are a much more common problem than is generally realised an affect a large proportion of the population. They can manifest themselves in many ways including agoraphobia, anticipatory anxiety, separation anxiety, school or work phobia. This book explains what Panic Attacks are, the causes, how panic affects daily life and the associated disorders. Conventional treatments together with their side effects are explained and alternative remedies including acupuncture, homoeopathy, reflexology, massage are covered. Karen Sullivan gives reassuring short term measures to help deal with an attack and, together with other advice, Top Ten Tips to help cope in the longer term.

ISBN: 1-903784-08-5

128pp

HOW TO COPE SUCCESSFULLY WITH

STRESS AT WORK

Beth MacEoin

In the UK we work longer and harder than our counterparts in Europe and America. Working under pressure has an adverse affect on our health and manifests itself in many cases as stress. It is now accepted that a reasonable amount of stress is a good thing and essential to motivate us and to trigger the 'fight or flight' response we sometimes need to deal with exceptional situations. Excessive stress can be extremely harmful and may in some cases cause death, for example the over pressurised Sales Rep speeding to their next appointment. This book contains positive strategies to solve these problems to break the negative cycle and enable you to re-assess your overall work situation.

ISBN: 1 903784-15-8

128pp